the
complete
candlemaker

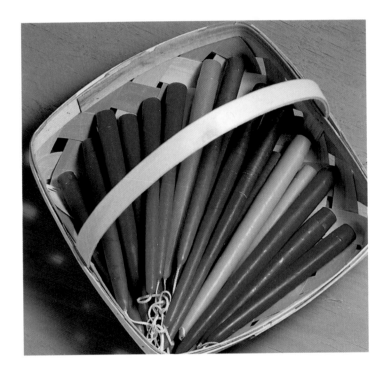

the complete candlemaker

- techniques
- projects
- inspirations

Lark Books

A Division of Sterling
Publishing Co., Inc.
New York

The book is dedicated to my husband Denny, who has always
encouraged and supported my creative efforts.

————————————————

Editor: Deborah Morgenthal
Assistant Editor: Laura Dover Doran
Art Director and Production: Celia Naranjo
Photographer: Richard Babb
Production Assistant: Bobby Gold

Coney, Norma J., 1955-
The complete candlemaker : techniques, projects, and inspirations / Norma Coney.
        p.   cm.
    Includes index.
    ISBN 1-887374-50-7
      1. Candlemaking. I. Title.
TT896.5.C66   1997
745.593'3—dc21   97-3615

CIP

10 9 8 7
Published by Lark Books, a division of
Sterling Publishing Co., Inc.
387 Park Avenue South, New York, N.Y. 10016

Distributed in Canada by Sterling Publishing,
c/o Canadian Manda Group, One Atlantic Ave., Suite 105
Toronto, Ontario, Canada M6K 3E7
Distributed in Australia by Capricorn Link (Australia) Pty Ltd., P.O. Box 6651, Baulkham Hills, Business
Centre NSW 2153, Australia
The written instructions, photographs, designs, patterns, and projects in this volume are intended for the personal use of the reader and may be reproduced for that purpose only. Any other use, especially commercial use,
is forbidden under law without written permission of the copyright holder.
Every effort has been made to ensure that all the information in this book is accurate. However, due to differ-
ing conditions, tools, and individual skills, the publisher cannot be responsible for any injuries, losses, and
other damages that may result from the use of the information in this book.

If you have questions or comments about this book, please contact:
Lark Books
50 College St.
Asheville, NC 28801
(828) 253-0467

Manufactured in the U.S.A.

ISBN 0-887374-50-7

contents

*intro*duction

A flickering flame has witnessed the history of the human race unfold. Primal man lived in a fearful world, but the ability to harness fire gave mankind the ability to ward off wild animals and the courage to face the darkness and the unseen perils of the night. In our century, methods of illumination have progressed considerably—electric night-lights now comfort children around the world.

Early tool makers were the first to utilize portable light; arrowheads and other necessities of life were made by firelight. For most of mankind, the transition from this crude method of illumination to a simple candle took centuries. As civilization advanced and ironworking was learned, *fire baskets* were used to make light transportable. These fire baskets, also called *cressets*, could be stoked with wood and kept alive for many hours.

Torches also made light portable. They were constructed of splits of resinous wood attached to the ends of long poles; the ends were dipped in tallow or waxes to add to their longevity. Fire baskets and torches were the only sources of public illumination for many societies. Enormous amounts of time, materials, and labor were expended to keep them burning.

One of the seven wonders of the ancient world, the Pharos of Alexandria or the Lighthouse of Alexandria, must have depended on means such as fire baskets and torches to beam its warning to ancient mariners. Built in A.D. 280 by Ptolemy II in honor of Alexander the Great, this marvel of antiquity stood at the delta where the Nile River meets the Mediterranean Sea. It has been estimated that this lighthouse stood 440 feet (135 m) tall. Imagine the effort put forth in order to keep its light burning! Today the remains of the lighthouse lie under the sea; the lighthouse fell victim to a series of earthquakes and finally was destroyed about A.D. 1400.

The use of fire baskets and torches for light may seem backward to modern people who merely flick a switch to illuminate a room. In fact, illumination was so precious in earlier times that all but the crudest lights and candles were reserved for ceremony, ritual, or religious purposes. Traditionally, the essence of a candle was the spiritual harnessing of fire. For centuries, the flame has symbolized hope, faith, eternity, and home.

Ancient pagan sun worshippers used candles in their rites and rituals. For instance, their winter solstice festivities included a "tree of light," sporting candles on the branches. This fertility tree was a precursor of our modern Christmas tree.

During the 19th century, candlelight traditionally was equated with domestic bliss in Greek festivities. On wedding days, candles were carried to the bride's new home by her mother and mother-in-law, and, with these candles, the "home fire was lit."

In centuries past, most people made their own crude "dips" or tapers from tallow—the white, solid, rendered fat of cattle and sheep. Beeswax candles were available, but they were far too expensive for the common man. In the Middle Ages the church was the primary user of beeswax candles. So many candles were used in church ceremonies that monetary endowments were sought to offset their cost.

During this period, beeswax was a precious commodity and candlemaking was an admirable trade to which a young man might be apprenticed. The Tallow Chandlers Guild was chartered in 1462 and the Worshipful Company of Wax Chandlers was chartered in 1484. At this time, it was a crime to adulterate wax in any way.

Even those far removed from the hub of activity in European cities yearned to extend the available daylight. In far-flung outposts where raw materials were few, people had to be resourceful in

order to obtain light. They achieved this by exploiting the natural resources at hand.

One of the more common ways to light the home was with a *splinter* or *rushlight*. Splinters were long, thin pieces of resinous pine that were spilt off the tree trunks, cut to a uniform length, and dried. These were clamped at an angle in a special holder made of wood or (preferably) metal.

Rushlights were used where pine was not available, particularly in the English countryside. The common or soft rush, called *Juncus effusus*, was cut in early autumn. The rush was soaked in water and then was peeled, dried, and dipped in fat. A rushlight measuring 2 feet, 4 inches (.7 m) would burn for a little less than an hour. Rushlights were placed in a special holder, lit at the upper end, and burned at an angle. Burned in this manner, rushlights were self-snuffing.

Some methods of obtaining light for the home were ingenious, albeit gruesome. In Western North America, locally caught candlefish were placed in a split stick and burned to provide light. In Newfoundland, fishermen split the tails of dogfish and burned the tails for light. In the Shetland Isles, wicks were thrust down the throats of storm petrels and the fatty birds were set ablaze. In other parts of the world, penguins and great auks (the latter is now extinct) were utilized in similar fashion. As primitive as these lighting methods may seem to us, they reveal the desperate need to provide light indoors during the evening hours.

American families who were able to make candles usually did so on the kitchen table. In all but the most affluent homes, these candles were made of tallow. The process was simple; several wicks were draped over a stick, then were repeatedly dipped into a large vat of tallow. This chore often was performed by the children of the house. Candlemaking was commonly done in conjunction with butchering, and each candle batch had to last until the next butchering. Even in the 19th century, purchased candles were a luxury. Most households made their own candles until the very late 1800s and some, no doubt, did so well beyond the 1800s.

The transition of candlemaking from the kitchen table to the factory occurred in the 1800s. At this time, candlemakers competed with soapmakers for the same raw material—tallow. These industrious people roamed the streets of

Avid Press, New Paltz, New Jersey

American cities in search of tallow, which they bought from housewives. Once these early manufacturers were established, they were often able to trade finished soaps or candles for the raw materials they needed to stay in business.

Proctor (a candlemaker) and Gamble (a soapmaker) first joined in the early 1840s in Cincinnati, a bustling city. There were 18 other soap and candlemakers in that city alone. Those

most successful were able to obliterate or buy out the competition. Some of today's largest corporations originated as manufacturers of candles and soaps, and then added other product lines.

Two major discoveries helped candlemakers move away from soft tallow candles to harder, longer burning, and more durable candles. First, in 1823, *stearin* was isolated from tallow, and candlemakers discovered that if an additional three or

Susan Schadt Designs, Del Mar, California

four percent stearin was added to the tallow, the candle burned more clearly and with less smoke than candles made from plain tallow. Stearin also had the ability to harden candles, an important consideration in warmer climates. Then, in the 1850s, paraffin was refined from petroleum for the first time. Paraffin burns brighter than tallow, and eventually could be manufactured in large quantities. In addition, paraffin wax was more easily released from molds than beeswax, which allowed for mass production of paraffin candles.

These refinements, coupled with a burgeoning candle market, allowed candlemaking to become an industry. Mass production of molds that could be filled, cooled, and released simultaneously also spurred the growth of the industry. Soon, all but the poorest or the most rural families stopped making candles at home.

Today, most people regard candles as an emergency provision, stored for times when power outages occur. Churches still burn candles for ceremonies and rituals, and many individuals buy candles to grace (often unlit!) the dining room table. But in the past few years, the practice of burning candles simply for the pleasure of the light they emit and the relaxing mood they create has increased dramatically. Evidence of this can be found in the tremendous variety of candle colors and shapes offered by upscale and discount stores. Home decorating magazines reflect and nourish this trend by regularly featuring articles that show the beautiful ways candles can accessorize every room in the house. Moreover, kits are now available that allow consumers to decorate a plain candle, or to roll their own beeswax candles and then embellish them. Some people are even exploring the heal-

Illuminée du Monde, Bristol, Vermont

ing effects of scented candles.

In light of this heightened appreciation of candles, it seems a propitious time to help people travel full circle…back to the time when folks made their own candles in their kitchens. My intention in writing this book is to provide, in a clear and inviting manner, all the information needed for you to make a variety of candles.

The book begins with a description of the basic equipment you will need to make candles at home. Next, you will find information about the wicks, waxes, and additives that go into the making of candles and give them their special properties.

Then you will learn about the wide variety of candle molds available today, the pros and cons of each, and how to prepare them for pouring. There is also a discussion of how to use ordinary household items, such as dairy cartons and juice cans, as candle molds.

The book also describes how adding fragrance and color can enhance your enjoyment of candles. Then there is a section covering work safety, time savers, and handy things to know, such as how to remove wax from the inside of your pots and pans, and how to make a dripless candle.

Then the book covers how to make the most popular types of candles: container candles, molded candles, and hand-dipped tapers. In these sections you will learn how to make layered, chunk, tie-dyed, hurricane, votive, and interior decorated candles. In the section on specialty candles you will be introduced to rolled beeswax tapers, hand-rolled spirals, water, sand, floating, and cut and curl candles. In special effects, you will find out

what it takes to overdip, marbleize, stipple, stencil, emboss, carve, appliqué, and more! This truly is a complete candlemaking book.

Candlemaking is fun and rewarding: there is something magical about repeatedly dipping a string into a pot of hot wax and watching a taper form in front of your eyes. As with any craft, practice does matter; the more candles you make, the better your results will be. But candlemaking is essentially easy—some candles can be made by children, under the supervision of an adult.

The flame of a candle is spellbinding, and it is easy to become mesmerized watching it dart and dance in the slightest breeze. Perhaps you feel a special connection to the history and symbolism of candles. Or perhaps candlelight reminds you of an era less hectic than our own. Whatever the attraction, I hope you will enjoy making your own candles. Perhaps your experience will light the way for others to follow.

candlemaking equipment

This section includes information on the basic equipment the home-based candlemaker needs. Information on molds can be found in Candle Molds on page 23. Supplies and equipment needed to make specialty candles or to create special surface effects are not covered here. For specific information on these items, consult the instructions in Specialty Candles (page 84) and Special Effects (page 102).

For the beginner, there are many questions to consider before buying equipment. Your budget, what types of candles you want to make, what

Clockwise from back center: commercial ladle, spoon ladles, mold weights, tea strainer, end former, kitchen knives in various sizes, scissors, awl, thermometer, hammer, rubber gloves, freezer paper, dipping frame, wick-centering spider, assorted cans

equipment you have on hand that may be converted permanently to candlemaking, and how serious you are about candlemaking as a continuing hobby, will all affect the decisions you make about purchasing equipment.

I have tried to sort out what equipment is most important for you to have and not cut corners on. When I began candlemaking, I did so on a shoe-string budget. I improvised as much equipment as I could and bought some basics to fill in the gaps. Eventually, I became frustrated with my improvised equipment. In candlemaking, there is much to be said for the old adage "the right equipment for the right job." The essential items you absolutely need to purchase are a wax melter, mold weights, mold sealer, and a mold holder for working with metal molds.

A complete list of required equipment is provided at the beginning of each of the following sec-

tions: Hand-Dipped Tapers, Candles from Molds, and Container Candles. I suggest you review these lists before you purchase any equipment so that you will have a better idea of what you need to make the candles that interest you.

Wax Melter. A good, durable wax melter is essential to the home candlemaker and is not the place to skimp. Wax melters are usually seamless aluminum; this prevents wax from being caught in the seam. The flat bottom allows the wax melter to sit right on the heat source, eliminating large, clumsy double-boiler setups. The sturdy handle allows a firm, steady grip for pouring hot, molten wax. I consider this to be the most important feature; a tenuous grip on a can of hot wax is not safe! If you can find an old stove-top coffee pot, it may serve you as well as a melting pot.

Candy or Wax Thermometers. A durable candy or wax thermometer is a necessity if you are to pour your wax at the proper temperature. When purchasing a thermometer, look for a long probe, a clip for hanging it on the side of a pot, and a scale that is large and easy to read. Critical temperatures to be read for candlemaking range from 150° to 300° F (66° to 149° C).

Dipping Vat. A dipping vat for tapers is an important piece of equipment. Galvanized vats are available at a depth of 15 inches (38 cm) and measure about 6 inches (15 cm) across. If you wish to dip long tapers, a dipping vat is a wise investment. If you will not be making many tapers and do not care about having long, perfect tapers, a dipping vat can be improvised. Juice cans, coffee cans, and various household items can be substituted. You will need a container 2 to 3 inches (5 to 7.5 cm) deeper than the length of taper you wish to make.

Also, make certain that the vat you choose is going to be wide enough to accommodate the width of your dipping frame, should you choose to use one.

Double-Boiler Bottom. When a double-boiler bottom is called for, do not take it literally! In fact, it would be a shame to damage a nice piece of kitchen equipment. A double-boiler bottom needs to accommodate cans of wax set in the container to melt. Expect the inside of the double boiler to get scraped up and—eventually—lined with wax. Essentially what you need is a pot—not too high and fairly wide (it has to fit on a large burner on your heat source). An old, seldom-used pot or a find at the thrift store will work nicely. I have had to resort to a 5-gallon (22.5 l) can to use as a double-boiler bottom for my large dipping vat, but this is necessary only when I am making long tapers on my dipping ring.

Dipping Frame. A dipping frame for tapers is a necessity if you want to make many perfectly straight tapers. Wick is threaded on the frame, which keeps the wick absolutely taut and helps avoid the sag that can occur when you dip tapers by hand. Dipping frames are available commercially or you can improvise by constructing the one detailed in Hand-Dipped Tapers, page 73.

Wick Holder. A wick holder is a simple alternative to a dipping frame. A wick holder made of wood, fitted with hooks to hold the wick, can dip two or three pairs of tapers at a time. Instructions for making a simple wick holder are found in the section on hand-dipped tapers, page 73.

Wick Rod. Wick rods are useful for holding the wick in place while the wax hardens. Often, wick rods come with metal molds; you can certainly use these with other molds or container can-

Several sizes of double-boiler bottoms are shown here, as well as a wax melter (center left) and a dipping vat (back left).

dles. A length of coat-hanger wire or a pencil work just as well.

End Former. This is a useful tool the professional candlemakers use to make a cleanly crimped end on tapers; this makes the tapers fit snugly in candle holders. Not a necessity, but nice to have.

Cool-Water Bath. A cool-water bath is a vessel in which cool water (not cold water) is placed in order to speed up the wax-cooling process. Cool-water baths must be scaled to the size of the candle you are making. They should be able to accommodate the entire length of the candle. If you are dipping tapers and are using a cool-water bath, it will need to be about the same size as the dipping vat you are using. If you are making molded candles, your cool-water bath must accommodate your mold.

Cool-water baths do not incur damage, and are best chosen when you choose your mold or taper length. Any pot, pan, or container (a bucket works for large molds) that is the correct size can be used. Never use your sink or bathtub directly as a cool-water bath (see page 42)!

Mold Sealer. Mold sealer is a pliable putty made specifically for sealing the wick holes in molds. Mold sealer works well, even if it must stick to wax or has some wax incorporated into it, making it worth its weight in gold to a candlemaker. Many manufacturers of molds include with the purchase of a mold enough mold sealer to seal one mold. It is always a good idea to have an extra stash of this invaluable material on hand. (Mold sealer is shown in the candle molds section on page 24.)

Mold Weights. Mold weights are long, flexible ropes of lead. Because they are flexible, they wrap around a mold easily. Mold weights are intended mainly for use with open-end molds, which would most likely tip—spilling the wax—when placed in a water bath. Two or three weights are sometimes required for a large mold.

Mold Holder. Mold holders are a good safety device that are used to pick up a large mold filled with hot wax and move it into a cool-water bath. Springs help keep the mold in place, and this lessens the danger of burning your hand or spilling

hot wax on yourself. I have found this device to be especially useful when working with large molds especially metal ones.

Piercing Device. A piercing device is needed to relieve the surface tension of the wax and to expose any hidden air pockets near the wick. A very thin, long knitting needle works well, as does a length of stiff wire or an awl. Your piercing device needs to be about as long as the wick on the candle you are making.

Wick Centering Spiders. You will often need a device to center the wick in the wax while the candle hardens. Some candlemakers chose to improvise and make these by hand, but I've found the top ring for a lamp shade frame (the washer-top style) works wonderfully. You can purchase these in a variety of sizes from a lamp shade supply company or take one from an old lamp shade you have around the house. If you get lucky, you might find exactly what you need at your local thrift store.

Assorted Odd Containers. This assortment can include cake pans, old ice-cube trays, bread pans, and any other similar items. They should be made of metal or tempered glass. You can accumulate these items as you need them. They are very useful to have on hand to pour wax into when you are finished working for the day. The wax then hardens, can be removed, wrapped, labeled, and stored so that it stays clean.

Old Frying Pan. This pan need not be large. It is used mainly to hold small containers of wax or dye safely on a burner when you are making some of the specialty candles.

Cans of Various Sizes. It is helpful to assemble several cans of different sizes. These are useful

to melt wax in (double-boiler style) when you do not have to pour the wax—for example, when making rolled appliqués. Any cans you set aside for this purpose should have sturdy seams and be clean and free of debris on the inside.

Small Tea Strainer. This need not be in mint condition but should be rust free. It is useful in helping clean debris out of wax (it happens to us all sometimes!) so that it can be used again.

Awl. A useful tool for punching holes in found molds, for widening holes, and for performing other useful procedures.

Mold-Release Spray. This silicone-based spray is used to coat the inside of molds to help the wax release from them.

Scale. A small scale is handy to have around your work station. It is especially helpful when you

need to estimate the overall weight of your wax and to calculate additives by percentage. (These tasks are difficult to do otherwise.)

Freezer Paper. Freezer paper helps keep your work surface clean or, as in my case, it keeps the wax clean if it is spilled. Having paper under the molds can save a lot of work later.

Old Towels. A small stack of old towels is good to have on hand. They can be used to insulate your work surface from a hot wax melter, hot molds, and so forth.

Rubber Gloves. Rubber gloves are used mainly for picking up hot items such as cans and molds. They have decent gripping ability and allow your hands some freedom of movement.

Solvent. A wax-removing solvent comes in handy at times because wax is so difficult to clean up. Look for one with chlorothene as its active ingredient from your supplier of candle equipment.

Spoon Ladles. Formed by simply bending a spoon to form

a ladle, these are extremely useful when working with odd-sized and small molds, particularly votive molds. Bear in mind that some spoons will break when you try to bend them, so do not be discouraged when this happens.

wicks, waxes,
and additives

This section is devoted to the physical ingredients that constitute a candle—the wick, the wax, and the additives that give candles special properties. Additives can affect the rate at which a candle burns. The size and type of wick also affect the burning rate. The quality and condition of the wax and its specific melting point play important roles, too. It is important for you to understand the properties of these essential candle-making materials and how each impacts the final

Nature's Creations, Creedmoor, North Carolina

product. This knowledge can help you figure out what went wrong if a particular candle burns poorly or does not live up to your expectations. However, it is important to keep in mind that candlemaking can be unpredictable. If you are a beginner, expect a period of trial and error.

WICKS

In days gone by, country folk (and sometimes city people) made their own wick. Today most people are not interested in making wicks—with good reason. Professional-quality wicks are readily available at very reasonable prices. Homemade wicks do not measure up to the tightly braided or wound wicks commonly found in today's marketplace.

Most candlemakers use three standard types of wick: flat-braided wick, square-braided wick, and wire- or lead-core wick. Each type of wick comes in several different sizes and each is used for a different type of candle. The size of the wick directly corresponds to the diameter of the candle you are making.

In most cases, you should put the wick in before you pour the wax, although sometimes (such as when making floating candles) the wick can be added after the candle sets up.

flat-braided wick

Flat-braided wick is used mostly for tapers. It can also be used for small pillar candles. Flat-braided wick looks like a flattened piece of string. It comes in sizes that indicate the number of plies or strands in the wick: 24 ply, 30 ply, 36 ply, and so on. The smaller the number, the smaller the wick, and the smaller the candle it is appropriate for.

square-braided wick

Square-braided wick is used primarily for block candles. The term *block candle* refers to a candle (either round or square) that is not a taper, but a large block of wax. The metal molds shown in the section on candle molds (page 23) are made to cast block candles.

In spite of its name, square-braided wick appears to be more round than square. It comes in numbered sizes: #1, #2, #6, and so on. The larger the number, the larger the wick. The smaller the wick, the smaller the diameter of the candle it is appropriate for.

wire-core wick

Wire-core wick is used for container candles and votives. As its name indicates, wire-core wick has a metal wire center. This allows the wick to stand upright under conditions that might make other wicks bend and drown in liquid wax. The available sizes that concern the home candlemaker are small, medium, and large. These sizes also correspond to the size of the candle.

priming the wick

Priming the wick for the candles you make is a good practice. Simply dip the wick into melted wax and coat it completely. Allow the wax to harden. Dip the wick into the melted wax again, and set it aside until you need it. This step accomplishes several things: 1) It ensures that the candle will light more easily. 2) Professionals will tell you that primed wicks burn more reliably. 3) Priming the wick prevents water or moisture from being absorbed by the wick; this is particularly important

Clockwise from back center: beeswax sheets, microcrystalline waxes (in both block and bead form), wick tabs, assorted wicks, beeswax, luster crystals, clear crystals, stearic acid, paraffin wax (large white block), USDA-grade beeswax, colored wax

if you make ice candles. Please note that in an effort to streamline the individual projects in the book, I do not include the step of priming the wick. However, it is a good habit and I recommend that you build it into your work routine.

WAXES

The discovery of paraffin wax in the 1850s brought this wax to the forefront of candlemaking by the late 1800s. Until the discovery of paraffin, natural waxes and fats were used for candles. In North America, bayberry wax and beeswax were most commonly used. In other parts of the world, people exploited available natural resources for other natural waxes, such as the wax derived from the tallow tree in China.

All these waxes have different characteristics. Some burn slowly, others burn quickly, some are mildly fragrant, others are not. In this book, we are concerned only with beeswax and the various types of paraffin wax.

beeswax

Beeswax is the wax that is taken from the hive of the honeybee. The honey is removed, the wax is cleaned, melted, strained of all debris, and is then ready to use. Beeswax has a natural golden color and sweet fragrance that has made it a favorite for centuries. Occasionally it is bleached to make it white.

Beeswax burns very slowly. It does not shrink when it hardens and therefore does not require topping off. One drawback to using beeswax to make candles is that the wax is soft and sticky and does not release well from molds.

paraffin

Paraffin wax is a by-product of the petroleum industry. It is a white semi-transparent hard wax that is suitable for a wide range of uses in candlemaking. It is not tacky and releases well from most molds. It is odorless and burns faster than beeswax. When you purchase paraffin wax, always be sure of its melting point. As shown in chart 1, the different melting points of paraffin determine what types of candles you should make from the wax. Usually the paraffin will be listed with a melting-point range; for example 140° to 145° F (60° to 63° C).

When you buy paraffin wax, make sure you consider the quality of the wax. Many inferior waxes are sold today. Get to know the going rate for the waxes you purchase and be wary of very

chart 1

melting point	*type of candle*	*flash point*
126°-131° F (52°-55° C)	container, hand-rolled tapers	approx. 410° F (210° C)
140°-145° F (60°-63° C)	tapers, block candles, sand candles	approx. 450° F (232° C)
154°-156° F (68°-69° C)	hurricanes, sand candles, overdipping	approx. 480° F (249° C)

Note: The *melting point* of a wax indicates the temperature at which the wax liquifies. The *flash point* of a wax indicates the temperature at which the wax ignites!

low prices. Generally you get what you pay for, and wax is no exception to this rule.

ADDITIVES

Over the years, there have been many materials added to wax to give it certain characteristics. Workability, slow rate of burning, added hardness, and opacity are a few desirable traits that additives can give wax.

A list of additives follows. If adding to the burning time of the candle is your only objective, then some of the additives listed will be interchangeable. Before doing much experimentation with candles, it is imperative that you understand what each of these additives is used for and how it is likely to affect the candles you make.

Stearic Acid. Discovered in the early 1800s, stearic acid is derived from tallow. It is a fatty acid that brings to wax the most desirable attribute of tallow—it adds to the hardness of the wax, giving it the ability to burn longer. Stearic acid also aids the ability of the wax to release from the mold by causing the wax to shrink slightly. Add stearic acid at a rate of 2 to 5 tablespoons (30 to 74 ml) per 1 pound (454 g) of wax.

Luster Crystals. Luster crystals have many useful qualities. This compound hardens the wax, adds to the burning time of the candle by raising the melting point, improves gloss or sheen, and brightens colors. It can replace stearic acid in any candle. Luster crystals should be used at 1 tablespoon (14.8 ml) per 1 pound (454 g) of wax.

Clear Crystals. Clear crystals also raise the melting point of the wax, thus adding to the hardness and the burning time of the candle. They also brighten colors and eliminate bubbles on the surface of the wax. Clear crystals are more translucent than most additives. All these attributes make them very useful when making hurricane candles. Use clear crystals at a rate of 1 tablespoon (14.8 ml) per 1 pound (454 g) of wax. One cup (200 g) of clear crystals per 1 pound (454 g) of wax can be used as an overdip to make your tapers absolutely dripless.

Microcrystalline Waxes. Microcrystalline waxes have become important in candlemaking. Their fine crystalline structure and opaqueness set them apart from paraffin waxes. They are powerful additives when used properly and each brings a particular quality to the wax.

You will find many varieties of micro waxes on the market; make sure you buy the one that will produce the results you desire. Different candle-supply sources use different names for these waxes. Chart 2 should help you purchase a micro wax according to the particular properties you want.

CARE AND STORAGE OF YOUR SUPPLIES

To keep your materials in good condition, they should be properly stored and handled. Though wax seems to be indestructible (unless you heat it),

it can develop problems in storage. Below are some guidelines for storing your waxes and wicks.

• Keep wicks packaged in plastic bags to prevent them from absorbing moisture. Always keep the manufacturer's label intact or make your own label that indicates the type and size of the wick stored in each package.

• Keep paraffin wax labeled to indicate the melting point of the wax. Wrap wax blocks in labeled plastic bags and store in a box. Keep away from light and moisture. Store in a cool location.

• Label all wax additives and store in plastic bags, snap-top containers, or similar airtight containers. Keep away from light and in a cool location.

• Be wary of rodent damage when you are storing wax—especially from mice, who can worm their way into even the nicest homes! Mice will eat wax, given the opportunity.

chart 2

wax type	tendencies	type of candle
Micro 170	Makes wax harder and less brittle	Hurricane
Micro 180	Eliminates internal bubbles	Hurricane, sand candles
Workable Micro (Sometimes called *white beads*)	Makes wax workable	Water candles, handrolled, cut-and-curl
Micro Tacky (May be called *sculpture wax*)	Builds layers of wax quickly, useful in appliqué because of tacky quality, "glues" wax to wax	Cut-and-curl, appliqué, overdipped
Micro Opalescent	Increases the interior glow, helps deter mottling	Container candles

candle molds

Clockwise from back center: mold holder attached to metal mold, assorted metal molds, corrugated material, plastic peel-back mold and plastic appliqué molds, polyurethane pop-out molds (green), found molds, mold sealer, wick rod, votive molds, found molds, two-piece plastic mold

Just a couple of decades ago, there were few mold choices for candlemakers. Due to the continuing popularity of the craft, a myriad of molds now exist. Today's molds are made from many different materials, but metal, rubber, and plastic are by far the best choices for candle molds.

Each type of mold offers certain advantages. Metal molds can be used to make large block candles with sharp, well-defined edges, while pop-out molds create details that are not possible with metal molds. The choice of molds for your candle-making endeavors depends solely on your personal preferences and your budget. As you begin to select molds, it is wise to try a variety of types and sizes so you can have the most flexibility and learn which types of molds you prefer to work with.

This section provides an overview of the vari-ous candle molds available today, including a dis-cussion of the pros and cons of each type of mold and how each is prepared for pouring. Because your molds are an investment that should last for many years, information has also been included to help you care for them and prolong their life.

METAL MOLDS

Metal molds are a candlemaker's standby mold. They are rugged, forgiving, and last for many years. Metal molds may be seamed or seamless. Unless you will be making dozens of candles, a seam in a candle should not influence your pur-chase because the line the seam makes on the fin-ished candle can be trimmed easily.

Metal molds are available today in a wide vari-ety of shapes and sizes. They are used mainly for making block candles. They leave a smooth finish on the wax. They are not the mold of choice if you are interested in making candles with patterns or textures because the molds lack detail. Metal molds are made by several manufacturers and may vary from each other slightly. If instructions are included with your mold, read them carefully.

wicking a metal mold

1. Remove the screw (if provided) from the wick hole in the bottom of the mold. Draw the wick through the hole in the bottom of the mold, up through the length of the mold, and out the top. Secure mold sealer (about the size of a quarter) to hold the wick on the bottom of the mold.

2. Cut the wick, leaving a few extra inches at the top. Wrap the extra wick around the wick rod (you can also use a length of coat-hanger wire

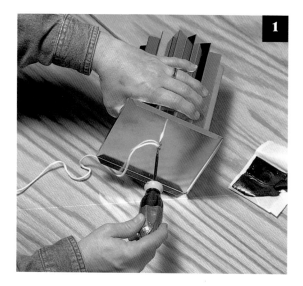

1

dle that comes from the mold and could affect how easily your candles release from the mold.

Metal molds should be kept in their original box when not in use. This keeps your mold dust free and prevents damage from falling objects and other mishaps.

Sometimes wax adheres to the inside of metal molds. This can come off on the next candle or prevent its release from the mold. The inside of metal molds can be cleaned in three ways:

or a pencil), which should be suspended across the top of the mold. Tie the wick firmly. The wick should be taut in the mold.

3. Replace the screw in the wick hole and screw it down tightly (photo 1). Make sure the mold sealer is secure on the bottom and that all the edges are pressed down tightly. Any crack that escapes your attention may let molten wax seep out of the mold.

4. You are now ready to pour the candle. Most manufacturers recommend that you run warm water on the outside of metal molds to warm them up immediately before pouring them. When you do this, be careful not to allow any water to splash into the mold or on the wick.

care of metal molds

Most metal molds are quite durable, yet some caution must be exercised to keep them in top condition. Dropping a mold can dent the surface, loosen a joint, or dent the end—devastating consequences for your mold. A slight dent will impact every can-

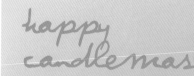

happy candlemas!

Candlemas (February 2) was originally a Celtic festival that celebrated the lengthening days of the year. It was one of the four days of the year representing a quarter of the calendar; on these days, witches practiced their Sabbaths. In Ireland and Scotland, these four days were celebrated as fire-feasts. February 2 was also the day that celebrated the return of spring. In the United States that day is known as Ground Hog Day. In Roman Catholic churches, Candlemas is the day that all candles to be used during the year are blessed. These candles are considered symbols for Christ as the light of the world.

Susan Schadt Designs, Del Mar, California

1. Rinse the mold with boiling water and wipe clean. Never do this over a drain; this is best done outside, if possible.

2. Pour your next candle in this mold at a temperature of about 235° F (113° C). This should remove any lingering wax without loosening the solder.

3. Clean the mold with candle-wax remover that has chlorothene as its active ingredient.

NOTE: Some candle molds have extremely sharp edges. When you get a new mold, you may wish to apply electrical tape to these edges (not the top rim of the mold). This will prevent you from receiving a painful cut when you pick up or move the mold.

PEEL-BACK AND POP-OUT MOLDS

These molds are recent innovations and provide the candlemaker a new dimension in detailed molded candles. Each type of mold is available in a wide array of shapes: animals, holiday themes, fruit, cut-glass objects, and much more.

Peel-back molds are made of heavy, flexible plastic. When the wax has hardened, the mold is peeled back on itself from the bottom until the candle can be removed.

Pop-out molds are made of molded rubber. Often these molds have slits in the sides. When the wax has hardened, these slits allow the end of the mold to open just enough to release the candle. Because the open end of these molds need not be large, they allow for remarkable detail, not only on the top of the candle, but on the sides. Read the manufacturer's instructions carefully before using these molds. Always handle these molds carefully because they will deteriorate over time.

wicking peel-back and pop-out molds

Peel-back and pop-out molds are wicked in the same fashion.

1. Peel-back or pop-out molds do not always have a wick hole, so you might have to make one. You can use either an awl or a tapestry needle to make the hole. If you use a tapestry needle, thread the wick through the needle. If you use an awl, you will need to poke the wick through the hole with the awl after the hole is made.

   Locate the center of the top of the mold—what will eventually be the bottom of the finished candle. Carefully and without piercing the sides of the mold, push the point of the tapestry needle or awl through the center of the top of the mold (photo 2, page 28). If you are using a tapestry needle, you may need to use pliers to pull the thread through the top.

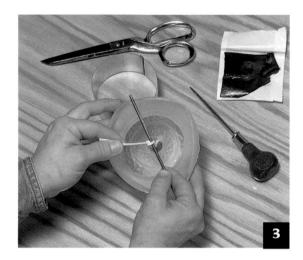

2. Remove the wick from the needle, leaving ¾ inch (2 cm) of the wick sticking out the top of the mold. Seal the top of the mold with mold sealer.

3. Cut the other end of the wick, leaving enough wick to tie around the wick rod. Tie the wick to the rod and place the rod across the opening of the mold (photo 3).

POURING PEEL-BACK AND POP-OUT MOLDS

The procedure for pouring peel-back and pop-out molds is essentially the same. In this example, we've used a pop-out mold and beeswax. *Never use beeswax for a peel-back mold.*

1. Before you pour the candle, place rubber bands around pop-out molds that have a slit in the side (photo 4). This keeps the side of the mold lined up properly and keeps hot wax from escaping.

2. Pop-out molds should be poured at 180° F (82° C) and peel-back molds should be poured at 190° F (88° C), unless the manufacturer recommends otherwise.

3. Peel-back molds will often need a mold stand because they have no support and the bottoms of the molds (usually the actual top of the candle) are not flat. A simple mold stand can be made with plastic containers or food cans fitted with plastic lids. Remove the lid from the can and cut a hole just large enough to prevent the mold from sliding through. The pop-out mold in photo 4, however, stands on its own.

4. In general, peel-back molds should be cooled using a cool-water bath. If you are using beeswax (only with a pop-out mold), allow the wax to cool slowly. Some manufacturers recommend that square peel-back molds be cooled in a warm-water bath. Follow the manufacturer's instructions. Often the mold stand you make can also serve as a cool- or warm-water bath.

Place the mold stand in a large bowl and fill the bowl with water. Whether the candle is poured before or after you place it in the stand (depending on the size and shape of the mold), be sure the water comes to the top of the candle.

5. Top off pop-out and peel-back molds as you would any other molded candle. Beeswax candles do not need to be topped off.

6. When the wax has hardened completely, remove the candle from the mold and trim the wick (photos 5 and 6).

care of pop-out and peel-back molds

Pop-out and peel-back molds should be kept in their original containers to prevent tears and other damage from occurring and to keep dust out of the interior of the mold. Any excess wax that remains in the mold can be removed by pouring boiling water in the mold (allowing the wax to soften) then pouring out the mixture (never into a sink or other inside fixture).

Peel-back molds will release more easily if they are allowed to cool completely and are then sprayed with a silicone mold-release spray. Never use solvents such as mold cleaner in these types of molds.

PLASTIC MOLDS

Plastic is often used in molds for candles that are flat (such as appliqué molds) or in two-piece molds. The plastics that are used for this purpose show a good amount of detail and are durable. The main disadvantage of plastic molds is that they develop warps over time; two-piece plastic molds can also be cumbersome to work with. Because plastic molds vary widely, I do not include information on wicking them. Each should be wicked in accordance with the manufacturer's instructions.

Bright Lights, Lower Lake, California

Molded beeswax candles by Illuminée du Monde, Bristol, Vermont

working with two-piece plastic molds

Two-piece molds require special handling if they are to produce attractive candles. The key in preparing two-piece molds is to get the plastic clamped together firmly enough to keep the wax from seeping out. Some two-piece molds will need to have a hole cut in one end. This hole is where the hot wax is poured into the mold. If you must cut a hole in your mold, follow the manufacturer's instructions and mark the hole in advance. Cut the opening with very sharp scissors to avoid cracking the plastic.

Depending on the mold, you may need to tape the wick to one of the plastic pieces, top and bottom, in order to hold it in place while the candle cools. Other two-piece plastic molds have wick holes and rods like standard molds. Follow the manufacturer's instructions exactly when position-ing the wick.

Many two-piece molds come with specially made plastic clips to hold the two sides together without any leaking. If your mold does not include these clips, heavy paper clips or paper clamps can be used instead. Some molds even come with a rubber gasket that fits between the two sides—this depends on the shape of the mold and the manufacturer. If your mold does not come with a mold stand, it is likely that you will be required to provide one while the candle is poured and while it is cooling.

Bright Lights, Lower Lake, California

One of the simplest mold stands is a box of clean sand. The mold can be snugly positioned, and will be supported by the surrounding sand. If the manufacturer does not recommend a pouring temperature, pour the candle at 180° to 190° F (82° to 88° C). Often two-piece molds will leave a seam of wax that will need to be trimmed off with a sharp knife.

care of plastic molds

Like any other mold, plastic molds should be stored in their original box to protect them from cracking, accidental damage, and dust buildup. To clean a plastic mold of excess wax, use a wax-removing solvent with chlorothene as its active ingredient. Do not pour it directly into the mold. Place solvent on a soft, clean cloth and wipe the affected surfaces until they are free of debris.

FOUND MOLDS

You may want to experiment with using com-mon household containers as candle molds. Some of my favorites include dairy cartons, cardboard juice cans, rigid plastic containers (shampoo bot-tles, etc.), cocoa containers (rigid cardboard), and cleanser containers. Sometimes the results with these molds are excellent and sometimes such molds fall short of expectations. Results are apt to be unpredictable, but there is little to lose by try-ing—you can always remelt a candle if it doesn't please you, and using a found container will not cost you anything.

You can expect the finish on the surface of the candle to be dull and generally inferior to what you would get with a purchased mold. Another drawback is that lines are often left on the surface of the wax. These drawbacks are not devastating and can be overcome with a little effort (see Special Effects, page 43).

Potential found molds have to meet some requirements. They need to stand up to the heat of the wax without melting, sagging, or springing a leak in the middle. They also must provide some means of securing a wick—you will need to poke a wick hole in the bottom of the mold. I reinforce dairy cartons by taping heavy cardboard reinforcements on the sides to prevent them from sagging. If you plan to throw away the found mold after one use, the top need not be larger than the bottom because the mold itself can be peeled or cut off and discarded after the candle has hardened. Containers such as cleanser cans are easily used as candle molds. Find the center of the bottom and punch a hole with an awl. Wick the mold as you would for any metal mold.

CORRUGATED OR MESH-FINISH MOLDS

Corrugated or mesh-finish molds are very attractive on a candle, but unfortunately most of us must improvise to achieve them because they are extremely difficult to find from candle-supply sources. To create these finishes, make an inner sleeve of needlepoint mesh or corrugated material about the same diameter as the found or metal mold that the sleeve will be set into for support. This technique is easier to manage with a mold that is less than 9 inches (23 cm) high.

Measure the outside of the mold you will be using to support the inner sleeve. Add 2 inches (5 cm) to this measurement. Cut a piece of corrugated material to the height of the mold you will

be using. Cut this piece to the measurement of the diameter plus 2 inches (5 cm). Generously coat what is to be the inside of the mold with silicone mold-release spray.

Roll the corrugated material around, making sure that the diameter is fairly even from top to bottom. Staple the material together and tape the

Two's Company, Mount Vernon, New York

seam with duct tape on the outside. Place the sleeve in the mold and wick the mold as usual (photo 7). If necessary for support, stuff the gap between the outside mold and the sleeve with rolled-up paper towels.

Pour hot wax into the bottom of the mold about ½ inch (1.5 cm) deep and allow to harden in the refrigerator. Remove and pour about 1 inch (2.5 cm) of wax into the mold and place in the refrigerator to harden around the outside edges. Remove from the refrigerator and pour the candle. Allow the candle to harden, topping it off as necessary.

When the candle has cooled completely, remove the sleeve from the mold. Slice open the duct tape and remove the staples. Open up the sleeve to reveal your candle. The bottom of the sleeve will have excess wax that seeped out of the sleeve into the mold. This will have to be trimmed in order for your candle to be attractive. The candle will also need to be leveled off.

For a mesh finish, secure needlepoint mesh to a flexible piece of cardboard and fashion a sleeve as for the corrugated candle on page 33. Proceed with the steps for making a corrugated candle.

D.L. Hill, Salt Lake City, Utah

Two's Company, Mount Vernon, New York

adding fragrance and color
to candles

Experimenting with fragrance and color is one of the joys of candlemaking. There is a wide variety of dyes and fragrances available, and a little imagination can yield endless possibilities.

FRAGRANCES

Many candlemakers believe fragrance to be one of the most appealing qualities a candle can have, and indeed scent can have a powerful effect. Fragrance has the ability to set the mood of a room and can, with one whiff, transport us back to childhood or to a specific time and place.

In recent years, scientists have studied the role of fragrance and have discovered some astonishing things. First, the sense of smell is indelibly imprinted in the human brain. When an odor is associated with memories, pleasant or unpleasant, even a hint of the scent will cause a recollection of these memories. Fragrances have other powers as well. Students who were allowed to sniff peppermint oil while taking exams did consistently better than they had done previously. Many other fragrances have been found to be soothing, stimulating, or healing. Thus, science is now beginning to support what herbalists have known for centuries.

fragrance oils

Fragrance oils are manufactured on a large scale for a wide variety of uses. Fragrance oils refer to oils that are synthetically made. In other words, they are not natural, but are developed in a laboratory.

As negatively as some purists will surely feel about synthetic fragrance oils, there are some advantages to using them. One is the astounding variety that is available. Fragrance oils can be made to smell like a coconut, an apple pie, an orange blossom, newly mown hay, or a famous perfume. They are available as a single fragrance or as a combination of fragrances. Another advantage is that, compared to their natural counterparts, fragrance oils are inexpensive and versatile.

Because of these advantages, most candlemakers use synthetic fragrance oils in their candles and, for all but aromatherapy candles, I believe synthetics are the best choice. They will increase your enjoyment of the candles you make and the oils are affordable.

essential oils

Essential oils are made from plant material. They are all natural and unadulterated. Most essential oils are quite expensive. Their high price is justified—it can take several hundred pounds of plant material to make a single ounce (28 g) of essential oil. For some types of essential oils, it takes one ton or more of plant material to make 1 ounce (28 g) of oil.

Clockwise from back: fragrance oil, essential oils, candle dye pieces, dye blocks in assorted colors

chart 3

relaxing	*stimulating*	*sensual*
frankincense	cinnamon	jasmine
myrrh	bergamot	rose
sandalwood	jasmine	vanilla
ylang-ylang	lavender	ylang-ylang
	peppermint	

Like fragrance oils, essential oils have their place. Because they are the very essence of the plant they are derived from, essential oils deliver powerful medicinal effects. They play an important role in aromatherapy.

aromatherapy candles

Aromatherapy candles are meant to deliver the power of essential oils as the fragrance of a gently burning candle is inhaled. These candles are designed to elicit the emotional and physical response associated with the essential oils they contain.

Aromatherapy candles are ideally made of 100 percent beeswax. Using beeswax is in keeping with the practice of using natural materials in the healing process. In aromatherapy, each scented candle elicits a specific response when its vapors are inhaled. Aromatherapy candles are labeled according to the responses they bring forth: relaxing, stimulating, and so on.

You can try your hand at making your own aromatherapy candles at home by using chart 3 above. It should be said that a little essential oil usually goes a long way. They will vary in strength from one to another. Use a light hand when adding them to your candles—you can always add more.

using fragrance oils in your candles

Fragrance oils differ in strength from manufacturer to manufacturer and from fragrance to fragrance. Therefore, it is not possible to provide a definitive formula to apply when scenting candles. However, most manufacturers of candle fragrances label their products to give a general idea of how many pounds of wax the particular fragrance will scent. If your taste in fragrance runs to the extreme, the scent may not last as long for you, but at least you will have a starting point.

You will notice that the instructions for making the individual candles do not include adding fragrance. I did this in an effort to streamline the instructions and keep them general. That being said, if you want to add scent, do so before you pour the wax.

using powdered herbs for gentle fragrance

As unusual as it may sound, you can use finely powdered herbs to add fragrance and color to candles. The key is to use the herbs sparingly. Powdered cinnamon, nutmeg, frankincense, and myrrh will add a subtle scent to your candles. In addition, these herbs will impart color and texture to the wax. Powdered cinnamon has been added to the candle in the foreground on page 35 to achieve a rich, brown color and a lovely fragrance.

Follow these simple guidelines when using powdered herbs.

• Make sure that the herbs are in fact very finely powdered. Large fragments may cause the flame to sputter.

• Use powdered herbs only in candles made from molds.

• Add the herbs to the wax just before you pour the wax into the mold. Make sure that the herb is evenly suspended in the wax. You can expect some settling of the powder at the bottom of the candle.

• Do not overdo! Too much material will cause sputtering or affect how well the candles burn.

CANDLE DYES

Color adds a lot to a candle, and I expect that you will want to make candles in a variety of colors. Candle dye blocks are readily available anywhere candlemaking supplies are sold. Dyes are also available in powdered form.

Candle dyes are not dyes in the traditional sense because they do not actually change the color of the wax. In fact, the dye pieces become suspended evenly throughout the wax, giving the illusion of color. Candle dye pieces are specially formulated so that the color will be distributed evenly.

Candles courtesy of Earth Guild, Asheville, North Carolina

Many people have become accustomed to using crayons to color candles, but I do not recommend doing this. Crayons are not formulated to suspend evenly throughout the wax. The color will sink to the bottom unless it is constantly stirred. Often crayons leave this sediment in the candle itself. Occasionally this sediment becomes drawn up by the wick, causing the flame to sputter.

The availability and economy of candle dyes make them the best choice for the home-based candlemaker. Candle dye blocks are very easy to use. The packaging should tell you how many pounds of wax each block will color. If you like intense colors, you can assume the block will not go as far as the manufacturer suggests. Scoring the blocks into quarters is the best way to divide them accurately.

Again, I have not included information on adding dye in the individual candle instructions in this book. In general, candle dye should be melted separately from the wax and from additives (also melted separately). This gives you more control over the amount of dye that is added.

After all the additives have been added to the wax and before the fragrance is added, you may add the dye and adjust the color of the wax to your liking. With a little practice, you can make simple combinations of primary colors to create delicate shades. White or black dye can also be used in combinations with colors to lighten or darken them.

safety, time savers, and handy things to know

Working with wax can be challenging. We all want to do our best to come up with a beautiful candle. Sometimes it is easy to become so caught up in the mechanics of what you are doing that you lose sight of what should always be in the back of your mind—safety.

Wax is flammable. A key to safety in any craft is knowing the limitations of what you are working with and what the consequences are if you go beyond those limitations. I have taught enough craft classes to say with confidence that you need to be cautious with—not afraid of—the materials you work with. With fear comes doubt, and when you doubt yourself, you are accident prone. By the same token, you should have a healthy respect for your materials.

Another key to safety is organization. To stay organized, you must become familiar with what you will be doing next, and you must establish a clear and sensible working order. To work efficiently, you need to concentrate on the task you are doing and also think ahead to the next steps you will be undertaking. It is a good idea to read through the instructions provided for each type of candle before you start to follow the steps. That way, you will stay organized, efficient, and safe.

Last, it is vital that you build safe habits into your working order. Learn what the risks are, then learn ways to avoid them. Build these avoidance techniques into your routine from the beginning, and they will always be your shutoff valve to problems.

Safety aside, there are always things to know about any craft that can save you time and energy. Short cuts, measurements, and sometimes things that seem obvious can save you a lot of trial and error. Read this section carefully before you make your first candle, and refer to it whenever you arrive at a roadblock.

SAFE WORK HABITS

Listed below are some rules to follow when you work with wax. Some of them may seem obvious, but it pays to read them anyway. An ounce of prevention is worth a pound of cure!

• Working with wax is time consuming. Set aside time or choose a time when you will not feel rushed. Many accidents can happen when you start cutting corners.

• Work in a large, well-ventilated space.

• Work in clothes you do not mind spattering with wax.

• Do not skimp on equipment. Working with makeshift items can create situations that put you and your loved ones at risk. In the equipment section (page 13) I list the equipment I consider absolutely necessary.

• Cover your worktable with clean freezer paper. This protects your work surface and helps keep the spilled wax free of debris so that it can be recycled.

• Never leave wax unattended on any heat source.

• When you are melting wax, it is essential to be able to put out a fire quickly should one occur. Always keep close at hand a lid that snugly fits your wax-melting pot. If the wax catches on fire, put the lid on the pot and immediately turn off the heat source. This should extinguish the fire. Pay particular attention to this safety practice if you are new to candlemaking and are using a wax-melting pot; the temperature of wax melted in this fashion can rise faster than you might imagine and accelerate to dangerous levels.

• When you are melting wax, keep a thermometer in it at all times. With a glance, you can check the temperature of the wax and know if you are in danger of reaching the flash point. The flash point varies for paraffin wax, but if you are over 300° F (149° C), you are in danger. Turn off the heat source and immediately remove the wax from it as safely as possible.

• Never try to put out a wax fire with water; this will just scatter the flames! Wax fires should be smothered with a lid from a sturdy pan or with a wet, heavy cloth or towel. Always keep these items handy—just in case.

• Clean up all wax spills as soon as they happen. This is especially true for wax spills on your heat source, particularly if it is your kitchen stove.

Chances are the burners have drip pans, and when the wax spills repeatedly in the catchalls, a

dangerous situation is created; the next time you turn that burner on a high setting, you will have a full-fledged kitchen fire. Wax spills on the stove can be cleaned up more easily if the stove surface is warm.

• When using a wax melter it is easy for small amounts of wax to drip down the outside of the pot as you pour and build up on the bottom of the wax melter. As a result, wax can accumulate under the burner and create excessive amounts of paraffin fumes in the air. To prevent this, wipe the bottom of the wax melter with paper towels after each time you pour.

• Keep pot handles turned in toward the rear of the stove to reduce the risk of you or someone else catching a sleeve on the handle and getting burned.

• Keep pets, children, and other potential distractions out of the work room while you are working.

• Never pour wax down a drain or create a situation in which it might accidentally go down the drain. Never place a candle directly into a sink or bath tub for a cool-water bath. The following true story will make you think twice before doing so.

A candlemaker was making a hurricane candle. It was poured and the mold was supposedly sealed with mold sealer. The candlemaker filled the sink with cool water and put the mold directly into the sink. The phone rang and a conversation ensued— away from the sink. When the candle was checked, there was no water in the sink—it had drained out—and there was no wax in the mold; the sealer was not tight or possibly had failed! The wax had run down the drain and into the septic system and leach field, clogging the works when it hardened. The bill came to about $1,500!

Two's Company, Mount Vernon, New York

TIME SAVERS

Time saving is a crafter's dream. It is not always possible, but once in a while we can do it. Here are some ways I have developed that save me time in my workshop.

• Generally wax is sold in large, heavy blocks which are difficult to break into useable pieces. To make the job go faster, simply place the block in a clean, sturdy cardboard box and give it a few good whacks with a good hammer. This is very effective (and also feels great if you are in a bad mood!). Store these smaller chunks in bags, being sure to label them so that you know exactly what kind of wax it is.

• Accurately calculating how much wax you need to pour to make a candle in a particular mold can be a time and wax saver. The following method is an easy way to estimate wax amounts. Plug the hole in the mold with mold sealer and fill it with water. Pour the water out, measuring as you go. For each 9 ounces of water in the mold, you will need approximately ½ pound (227 g) of wax. Dry the mold thouroughly.

• When you are finished for the day, there is always extra wax left over. Do not leave this wax in your wax-melting pot! Have handy some second-hand (but clean) pans and pour the leftover wax into one of the appropriate size. Make a tag, detailing what fragrance the wax is, what melting point, and what additives have been used in it. These notations will come in handy when you need wax for a project down the road and will ensure that you do not use the wrong wax for the job. When the wax hardens, wrap it in plastic and position the label so that it can be easily read.

• Making wax chunks for chunk candles requires pouring the wax into an old, clean baking pan. Sometimes the wax can be a bit tough to remove. To prevent this, oil the pan first with a spray of vegetable oil that you would use in the kitchen. The wax should then lift right out of the pan.

HANDY THINGS TO KNOW

This is a collection of tips and reminders for you to use as a reference. It includes some things that have been included elsewhere and some that never found a place in other sections.

Removing Seams on a Candle. Some molds will leave a noticeable seam line on the candle. These lines are easily removed. Hold a paring knife almost at a right angle to the candle on the seam. Turn the candle or use a smooth motion with the knife until all the extra wax has been removed. The remaining marks can be buffed off with a nylon stocking.

Cleaning Soiled Wax. If you work with wax long enough, it will happen—you will end up with dirty wax or sediment in the wax. Your wax can probably be saved. Melt the wax over water in a small can. Cut a couple of thicknesses of clean muslin cloth and place them in a small tea strainer. When the wax is hot, pour it slowly through the tea strainer into an old baking pan or similar item. Allow to harden, checking the bottom of the wax. If there is any sediment left, repeat this process or simply scrape it off the bottom.

Cleaning Soiled Candles. Soiled candles can often be cleaned with a soft nylon cloth and a little elbow grease. Buff the candle lightly with the cloth. If the dirt is stubborn, try putting a tiny drop of mineral oil on the cloth and buff again. Candles with dull surfaces can sometimes be buffed to a better surface using this process.

Making Molds Go Further. Metal molds in particular can be used to make several different sizes of candles. I always buy the tallest mold offered of a particular diameter. Using the same mold, I can make tall candles the full height of the mold, or I can make shorter candles by filling the mold less full. For efficiency, wick as usual, tying the wick to the rod, but do not cut off the wick—leave it attached. This leaves all the extra wick intact for another candle.

When you pour the wax, try not to drip any wax on the inside walls of the mold above the candle's height because this extra wax makes it harder for the candle to release from the mold. Keeping the wax off the walls of the mold is easier to accomplish when you work with larger diameter candle molds. To remove this wax, simply trim the drips at the height of the candle right after the drips harden, then peel off the rest of the wax with a knife.

Distorted Color. Working with candle dyes is a lot of fun, but sometimes the color becomes distorted. Why does this happen? Colors become distorted when the temperature of the wax rises too high. Temperatures over 225° F (107° C) can damage some colors, so, for best results, keep the wax at recommended pouring temperatures.

Stubborn Wicks. Sometimes a wick is just a bit too limp or stubborn to go through a wick hole. To make the job easier, dip the end in melted wax, let cool just a bit, and roll it between your fingertips. The wick should then go through the hole with room to spare. Another way to solve this problem is to prime the wick (see explanation on page 19).

Wax on the Inside of Pots and Pans. When you use double-boiler setups for some of the procedures in this book, wax is sure to find its way into your pans. This really bugs me, because the next time the pan is heated, the wax will melt and coat everything in the pan with a film of wax. To get wax off my pans (and sometimes other things), I boil some water in my tea kettle and take the kettle and the pan outside. Pour the water over the wax and it will come off nicely. (The wax doesn't do much for the grass, so this is better done where grass is not important.)

Wax Removed from Other Surfaces. Solvents are available to help remove wax from some items, but you need to read the directions because they can not be used on all surfaces. Look for a solvent with the active ingredient chlorothene. Some wax can be removed from fabrics by applying ice until the wax becomes brittle enough to fleck off.

Warped Candles. It happens all the time—candles become warped in storage or possibly your hand-rolled candles do not set up as straight as an arrow. There is a simple solution that works most of the time for me. Place the candles on freezer paper, then on a heat source that is not hot, but warm. For example, I put them on top of my 30-cup coffee pot for several hours. There is no danger of them melting there, because it is not that hot. After a few hours, the candle has been warmed sufficiently. Remove it and the paper from the heat and roll on a flat surface until the warp rolls out. Flared candles can be straightened by suspending them from the wick end. Caution: Do not place the candle on heat unless you are sure it will not melt!

Stuck Wax. Stuck wax in your candle molds can prevent the candles from coming out! Stuck wax can be removed easily from molds. For help with this problem, refer to the section on candle molds (page 29) for details on how to clean each type of mold.

How to Glue Wax to Wax. Whether you are applying appliqués or constructing a unique candle from scratch, being able to affix wax to wax surfaces can be a real benefit. It is easy to do with a fine microcrystalline wax that is tacky when melted, then dries to a hard surface. Just melt a little of this wax in a can and apply to both surfaces with an old, small paintbrush.

Candle Dripping Problems. Do your candles drip, no matter what you do? The solution is at hand: melt 1 cup (200 g) of clear crystals in 1 pound (454 g) of wax and dip the entire surface of your candle in this mixture. No more dripping!

Make Your Candles Burn Longer. It is easy to make your candles last longer. Stearic acid, luster crystals, and clear crystals will all do the trick. There is no need to use more than one of these additives, but one can be substituted for the other. For the rate at which you add them and other information, see the section on additives (page 21).

Making a Mold. You can improvise to create a mold for a candle shape you like even if no mold exists. To do this create a sand pit in a dishpan, as described for sand candles in the section on specialty candles (page 94). Sculpt your mold out of the sand by hand or by using an object similar in shape to your desired mold. Melt wax and pour it into the impression in the sand at 150° to 160° F (66° to 71° C). When the wax has hardened a little, place a thick wire in the wax where the wick will be inserted later.

When the wax is completely cool and removed from the sand, little or no sand will cling to the wax, because the pouring temperature was so low. Any excess sand can be brushed away. Insert the wick, and you have a candle of your own design.

not spaghetti— spermaceti!

During the great age of whaling, from the 1600s to the mid-1800s, *spermaceti*, the crystalline fat from the head of the sperm whale, was used as fuel in special lamps. Early mariners mistook this substance for sperm and named the whale accordingly. Spermaceti was so universally used that it became a standard measure—one candle power is equal to the light given off by a spermaceti candle weighing $1/6$ of a pound and burning at the rate of 120 grains per hour. Spermaceti was often mixed with ten percent beeswax to make candles.

Illuminée du Monde, Bristol, Vermont

container candles

Container candles have enjoyed enormous popularity in recent years, perhaps because they are extremely versatile, attractive, and functional. When not in use, they can become decorative accents in your home or can be easily covered and stored. Container candles are particularly appealing to collectors and recyclers, because they transform some of your household clutter into beautiful and functional candles!

When searching for candle containers, use your imagination. Many discarded household items cry out for a second life as a container. In order for a container to successfully accommodate a candle, however, a few requirements need to be satisfied. The container's opening must not be too small (anything smaller than 2 inches [5 cm] in diameter would be too hard to light), the material from which it is made must be able to withstand the pouring temperature of the wax and be nonflammable, and the container must be able to stop the flow of the wax.

Examples of candle containers are countless: attractive perfume vessels, old, rustic-looking tins, small decorative bowls, crockery, terra-cotta pots, mason jars, candy jars, and even shells may be used to house candles. The key to making good container candles is using the proper wax formulation.

In addition, wick tabs and wire-core wicking replace regular wicking techniques and allow the wick to stand erect in the container.

WAX FORMULATIONS

A paraffin wax with a low melting point is best for container candles. The ideal melting point for the wax or combination of waxes is 128° F (53° C).
- 50 percent paraffin, 131° F (55° C) melting point
- 50 percent paraffin, 126° F (52° C) melting point
- ½ ounce (14 g) of micro opalescent wax for each pound (454 g) of wax

WICKS AND WICK TABS

Wire-core or lead-core wicking is a special type of wick that has a stiff wire as its center. The stiffness of these wicks allows them to stand upright in situations in which another wick might fall over and extinguish itself. Wick size will vary with the diameter of the container you use for each candle.

Wick tabs hold the wick to the bottom of the container while the wax is poured and help to keep the wick upright. Tabs are available in several sizes. Choose them based on the size of your container: Use small wire-core wick for containers under 2 inches (5 m) in diameter, use medium wire-core

Four-wick container candle in center front is courtesy of Dollywood, Pigeon Forge, Tennessee.

wick for containers 2 to 4 inches (5 to 10 cm) in diameter, and use large wire-core wick for containers 4 inches (10 cm) in diameter and up.

POURING TEMPERATURE

Container candles should be poured at 160° to 180° F (71° to 82° C). Warm the container just before you pour the wax. To be safe, test glass containers ahead of time by placing them in a sink, warming them with hot tap water first, and then filling them with near-boiling water. If the container holds up to this, it should be safe to use as a container. Wax poured into glass containers should be poured at 160° F (71° C).

materials

Paraffin wax, 130° F (54° C) melting point

Paraffin wax, 126° F (52° C) melting point

Micro opalescent wax

Candle dye and fragrance*

Wire-core wick

Wick tabs

Container of your choice

Small tin can

equipment

wax melter

candy thermometer

mold sealer

wooden spoon

coat-hanger wire or wick rod

coat-hanger wire as long as your container

newspaper or an old towel

rubber gloves

*optional

instructions

When pouring container candles, avoid spilling wax on the outside of the container, as it can be difficult to remove from some surfaces.

1. Melting the wax: Place wax or waxes in the wax melter with the microcrystalline wax (if you are using it), then put the melter on your heat source on a medium setting.

2. Making final adjustments to the wax: Stir waxes together thoroughly. Bring the temperature of the wax to 160° to 180° F (71° to 82° C). Melt dye in a separate can and add to the wax. Add fragrance, if desired, and stir both dye and fragrance in completely.

3. Preparing the wick and tab: If your container has a hole in the end, such as a terra-cotta pot, secure it with mold sealer. Cut a sufficient length of wick for the container—with some extra to wrap around the coat-hanger wire or wick rod. Prime the wick (see page 19). Secure one end of the wick in a wick tab. As soon as the wax has melted, pour a small amount into the bottom of the container.

    Using the longer coat-hanger wire, press the wick tab firmly into the wax (photo 1).

Pour enough wax into the bottom of the container to securely cover the wick tab and allow it to harden into place. This will keep the tab secure while you are making any adjustments with the wick after pouring the wax. Position the wick rod across the top of the container, then wrap the other end of the wick around the support.

4. Pouring the candle: Put a rubber glove on the hand that will be holding the container; this will insulate your hand from the hot container when the wax is poured. Warm the outside of the container by holding it under warm tap water. Make sure that you have an old towel or newspaper on which to place the container once it has been filled.

    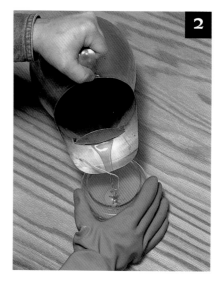

    Pick up the container in one hand, tipping it slightly. Pour the melted wax into the container, filling it to the neck of the container (photo 2, page 49). Adjust the wick to be certain it is centered.

5. Topping off the candle: As the candle cools, a well will form just as in a molded candle. (How long this takes depends on the size of the container, so check the candle every few minutes.) When the well forms, pierce the wax around the wick with the longer coat-hanger wire, piercing all the way to the bottom. Bring the wax back up to the pouring temperature and fill the well. Repeat this until a well no longer forms. Allow the candle to harden. Trim the wick to ½ to ¾ inch (1.5 to 2 cm).

Candles molded to fit inside tin containers by Two's Company, Mount Vernon, New York

Pei-Ling Becker, Black Mountain, North Carolina

molded candles

Advances in mold making now allow us to make intricately detailed candles that, at one time, crafters could only dream of. Candle molds come in many shapes and sizes and are made from a variety of materials. Metal, plastic, and flexible pop-out molds are readily available from candle supply companies.

With a little imagination, you can turn any number of household items into candle molds. Orange juice containers, cleanser cans, and dairy

Nature's Creations, Creedmoor, North Carolina

Two's Company, Mount Vernon, New York

cartons work well. A small selection of purchased molds and found molds should offer enough options to satisfy the most discriminating crafter. To ensure the longevity of your molds, however, proper care is essential (see pages 25, 29, and 32).

Making molded candles is perhaps the easiest form of candlemaking to learn, and it is a good starting point for children and beginners. Your results can be spectacular, the time investment is minimal, and you will reap hours of enjoyment from your labors. Also, molded candles are less demanding than fine tapers, in respect to both time and equipment.

Whether you are using a found mold or a commercial mold, the basic techniques for molded candles are the same. Most of the time commitment in making molded candles is in the initial melting of the wax and waiting for it to harden in the mold. One step you can take to reduce the time is to use a cool-water bath. Cool-water baths

also improve the finish of candles by making them smoother. You can also save time by planning ahead to make several molded candles from the same wax once it is melted.

WAX FORMULATIONS

Molded candles may be made from a large number of wax formulations, many of which contain additives for special effects. Because it is easy to get carried away when using additives, try experimenting with one additive at a time so that you can be certain of its effect on the finished candle. Paraffin wax is the easiest wax to use for molded candles. If you use 100 percent beeswax, it will easily release from pop-out molds but not metal molds. If you plan to use beeswax in traditional molds, you must mix the beeswax with paraffin.

Here are several reliable formulations.

1. 100 percent paraffin, 140° to 145° F (60° to 63° C) melting point
2. 100 percent paraffin, 140° to 145° F (60° to 63° C) melting point, with 5 tablespoons (74 ml) stearic acid and 1 teaspoon (5 ml) luster crystals added per pound (454 g) of wax
3. 50 percent paraffin, 140° to 145° F (60° to 63° C) melting point, 50 percent beeswax
4. 100 percent beeswax

Estimating in advance the amount of wax you need to fill a certain mold has obvious advantages. Many manufacturers include this information with individual molds. If this information is not available, you can estimate the amount of wax you will need using the following method: Fill the mold with water. Pour the water out and measure how much it took to fill the mold. Each 9 ounces

Bright Lights, Lower Lake, California

(252 g) of water equals approximately 8 ounces or ½ pound (227 g) of solid wax. Be sure to thoroughly dry the inside of the mold.

WICKS

It is important that you choose the right wick for molded candles. The wick must be appropriate for the wax formulation and the size of the candle.

Wax formulations can affect wick performance. Additives such as stearin and luster crystals extend the burning time of the candle. This, in turn, influences how the wick performs. Therefore, you may need to adjust the wick size as necessary. The quality of the wax used in the candle will also have a significant effect on how the wick burns.

Chart 4 suggests wick sizes for various molded candle diameters, including both flat-braided (F.B.) and square-braided (S.B.) wicks. The recommendations are based on wax formulations and candle diameters. If your candle does not burn properly, you will need to consult the troubleshooting guide on page 119.

POURING TEMPERATURES

These recommendations for the pouring temperature of wax are general. Many times manufacturers include instructions that include pouring temperatures with specialty molds. Manufacturer's recommendations should always be followed.

For metal molds: pour wax at 200° F (93° C)

For plastic and acrylic molds: pour wax at 180° to 190° F (82° to 88° C)

For rubber molds: pour wax at 190° F (88° C)

For 100 percent beeswax candles: pour wax at 170° F (77° C)

For cardboard found molds: pour wax at 190° F (88° C)

MAKING MOLDED CANDLES

The following lists specify the materials and equipment you need to make molded candles.

materials

Paraffin wax, 140° to 145° F (60° to 63° C) melting point

Stearic acid (do not use for rubber molds)*

Luster crystals*

Wick, enough for the candle plus a few extra inches (5 cm)

Candle dye*

equipment

Wax melter

Candy thermometer

Wooden spoon

Rubber gloves

Cool-water bath*

Mold of your choice

chart 4

candle size	wick size
1–2 inches (2.5–5 cm)	F.B. 15 or 24 ply, S.B. #5/0
2–3 inches (5–7.5 cm)	F.B. 30 ply, S.B. #2
3–4 inches (7.5–10 cm)	F.B. 30 ply, S.B. #3
4–5 inches (10–12.5 cm)	F.B. 30 or 36 ply, S.B. #3 or #4
5–6 inches (12.5–15 cm)	F.B. 45 ply, S.B. #5
6–9 inches (15–23 cm)	S.B. #6
Beeswax/paraffin candles	S.B. #1 or #2
Beeswax candles over 2 inches (5 cm) in diameter	S.B. #4 or #5

Bright Lights, Lower Lake, California

Mold stand, purchased or improvised (to hold flexible molds during pouring)

Mold sealer

Mold weights

Mold holder (makes it easier to move large metal molds to the water bath)*

Wick-centering spiders*

Coat-hanger wire as long as the mold or a long, thin knitting needle

Coat-hanger wire or wick rod

Old metal pie pan

*optional

instructions

Establish the following working order when you set up to make molded candles. If you are a beginner, make sure you read the safety precautions and time-saving tips in the section on safety (page 40) before you begin.

1. Setting up to melt the wax: Place the wax (in the formulation you have chosen) in the wax melter. Put any additives in other containers and melt them separately. Place the melter on your heat source and heat it on a moderate setting. Position a thermometer in the melter.

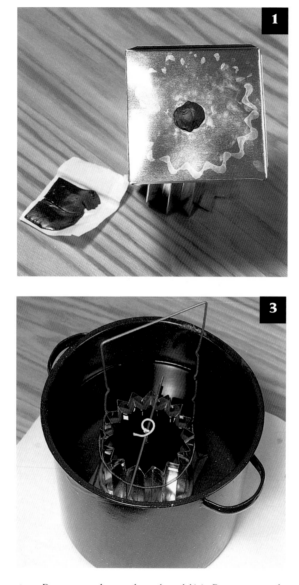

2. Preparing the wick and mold(s): Prime enough wick for the mold(s) you want to pour. Primed wicks will light much easier than those that have not been primed. To prime the wick, see the section on wicks, waxes, and additives (page 19).

Wick the mold. Make certain that the wick hole is completely sealed with mold sealer (photo 1). For complete information on wick-

ing and preparing the mold, see pages 24 to 26. Metal molds should be warmed by running warm water over the outside of the mold before the wax is poured. If you are using a metal mold, attach the mold holder at this point. If you will be placing the mold in a cool-water bath, be sure to attach mold weights to the bottom of the mold at this point.

3. Set up a cool-water bath: If you are using a cool-water bath, it should be deep enough to accommodate the entire length of the candle. It is a good idea to set the cool-water bath in a sink for ease of emptying it when you are finished, but NEVER use your sink or tub directly as a cool-water bath. You should not use a cool-water bath for beeswax candles.

4. Final adjustment of the wax and additives: Check the temperature of the wax as soon as it has melted and bring it to the correct pouring temperature. When the wax reaches the correct pouring temperature, add the additives, fragrance, and dye, stirring them into the wax thoroughly.

5. Pouring the candle: You might want to wear rubber gloves to insulate your hands from the heat when you pour the wax. With one hand, tip the mold slightly. Slowly pour the liquid wax into the mold until the mold is filled to the desired depth (photo 2). Reserve a small amount of the wax for the topping-off process. Adjust the wick to make sure that it is correctly centered in the mold. Allow the filled mold to sit for two or three minutes, then tap all around the sides gently, but firmly, with a wooden spoon. This removes air pockets or bubbles that can sometimes form on the sides of the molds.

6. Carefully place the mold in the cool-water bath (photo 3). Make sure that the mold is properly weighted and that it will not tip. If you have made a beeswax candle, skip the cool-water bath and move on to step 7.

7. Special instructions for beeswax molded candles: This step is only for candles made from 30 percent or more beeswax. Beeswax needs to cool very slowly, and so cannot be placed in a cool-water bath. If they cool too quickly, these candles will have a tendency to develop large cracks as they harden. To slow down the cooling process, place the mold in a container that can be covered. A crock, glass mixing bowl, dutch oven, cardboard box, or plastic container will work as long as it can be covered. The idea is to keep the heat from escaping quickly. If you do not have a container large enough, place the mold in an out-of-the-way location and carefully cover it with a heavy towel.

8. Topping off the candle: Paraffin wax candles need to be topped off because the wax shrinks significantly as it cools. This shrinkage forms a deep well and submerged air pockets in the center of the candle. These need to be refilled with liquid wax. The time it takes for the well to form depends on the size of the candle, so it is best to check it every ten minutes or so. Candles with a larger diameter may take up to 45 minutes before the well is evident.

   When a well has formed in the center of the candle, it can be topped off. First, heat the reserved wax to the correct pouring temperature. Using a wire or knitting needle, pierce the wax directly around and down the entire length of the wick several times (photo 4). (This allows any submerged air pockets to be filled.) Fill in the candle with the reheated wax (photo 5). Be sure that you do not pour the wax any higher than the original wax in

the mold, as this will make the candle harder to remove. Large paraffin candles may need to be topped off two or three times. When a well no longer forms, allow the candle to harden overnight.

9. Removing the candle and finishing the base: Untie the wick from the open end of the mold and remove the mold sealer and/or screw from the other end. Candles made from metal molds may be placed in the refrigerator for an hour to help make them easier to remove. Gently tap the mold against your hand until the candle emerges (photo 6). Trim the wick on the top of the candle to ½ inch (1.5 cm). Trim the wick on the base of the candle as close to the wax as possible. If the candle base is not level, put it, with its base down, on an old pie plate, then place the plate on a warm burner (photo 7). The offending wax will melt away and your candle will be perfect!

VARIATIONS OF MOLDED CANDLES

The techniques listed below are ways to easily manipulate the color or texture of a molded candle as the candle is poured. Unless otherwise noted, use wax formula #1 or #2 listed in the beginning of this section (page 52) to make these variations of molded candles. Refer to the materials and tools list on page 13 for general supplies. Any additional supplies specific to these candles are cited in the individual instructions.

LAYERED CANDLES

Layered candles are made by pouring wax (possibly left over from other projects) in layers.

You can also create a simple layered candle by overdipping a candle in a single color at various levels. In the latter method, the candle is immersed to a different level with each dip, making each layer slightly darker than the one before. The result is an attractive layered candle in shades of the same color (see pages 103 to 104).

Sue Teckow, Asheville, North Carolina

I have found that poured layered candles work best if made in metal molds. This is because the wax releases more easily; a well-intentioned tug on a layered candle can sometimes separate the layers. The following instructions describe how to pour layered candles.

additional supplies

Candle dyes in one or more colors

instructions

1. Follow instructions for making molded candles (page 54), omitting the cool-water bath. Melt the wax, adding the dye of your choice.

2. Pour the wax into the prepared mold. Be certain that none of the wax drizzles down the inner surface of the mold as you pour. If this happens, it can mar the layered effect. If you want to create an angled layered candle, carefully tip the mold, and secure it so that the wax can harden in this tipped position. Keep the wick centered at all times.

3. As the wax hardens, melt the next color of wax. When the first wax has begun to skim over, you can gently pour the second wax in. If you are angling the layers, you can change the angle of the mold at this point, if desired.

4. Repeat this process until the last layer is poured on the level. Top off, cool, and remove as you would any other molded candle.

ICE CANDLES

Ice candles are another fun variation of molded candles. They are not only a joy to make, but a pleasure to watch as the lacelike wax patterns formed by the ice slowly burn. When making ice candles, it is best to use crushed ice; large chunks make gaping holes in the wax, which can make the candle unstable.

additional supplies

Crushed ice (pieces ¾ inch [2 cm] in diameter work best)
Spoon

instructions

1. Follow the instructions for making molded candles (page 54), omitting the cool-water bath. Melt the wax and additives and bring them to the proper temperature.

2. There are two methods of securing a wick for an ice candle:

   Method #1: Wick the mold as usual. When the ice melts in the mold from the heat of the wax, some of the wick may become wet or damp, causing sputtering when it is burned. If you make the candle using this method, you can prevent sputtering by priming the wick, or allowing the candle to cure or dry for several weeks before you burn it.

candlelight for the soul

Medieval French cemeteries had stone towers that resembled lighthouses and were called "lanterns of the dead." Candles in these towers were lit at the moment of a person's death and remained lit until after the funeral. Their purpose was to light the way for the departing soul.

Method #2: Prepare the mold, omitting the wick. In place of the wick, put a taper or block candle (depending on the diameter of the mold for the ice candle) in the mold, cutting it to the correct height to match the height of the mold. Run the wick from the taper through the wicking hole in the mold and seal as usual, or adhere the taper to the bottom of the mold with some melted wax. There is only one drawback to making an ice candle in this way: if the size of the wick in the taper does not take into consideration the ultimate diameter of the ice candle, the wick will tend to burn a hole down through the center of the candle.

3. Spoon crushed ice into the mold, bringing it just to the top of the mold (photo 8). Pour the melted wax over the ice until the mold is filled. When the wax has hardened completely, remove the candle from the mold over a sink; all the melted ice will drain away. You will now have a unique candle with holes where the ice once was. Allow the candle to dry completely before you light it.

candles for king tut

Torch holders were found In King Tut's tomb. These holders at one time held lengths of ropes that were treated with fats or oils. Archaeologists also believe that Egyptians of this period (1300 B.C.) used candles that resembled tapers.

Wax Wares, Asheville, North Carolina

CHUNK CANDLES

Making chunk candles is another great way to use leftover bits of colored wax. These candles are extremely attractive and can be made in either a single color or multiple colors.

additional supplies

Small amounts of several colors of candle dye

Shallow pan or old ice-cube tray

Sharp knife

Propane torch*

*optional

instructions

1. Melt the scraps of colored wax and pour each color into a shallow pan or old ice-cube tray to a depth of about ¾ inch (2 cm). When the wax has hardened but is still warm, score the top. I like to make chunks about ¾ to 1 inch (2 to 2.5 cm). This size works well for candles under 6 inches (15 cm) in diameter. For large candles, you may wish to make larger chunks. When the wax is hard enough, cut it into chunks.

Wax Wares, Asheville, North Carolina

2. Follow the instructions for molded candles (page 54). For the candle itself, use wax formula #1 with no additives. This protects the clarity of the wax so that you will be able to see the colored chunks more easily.

3. Prepare and wick the mold and place the chunks in the mold from the bottom to the top, making sure that many of the chunks touch the side of the mold (photo 9). Pour the melted wax over the top of the chunks until the mold is full. Place in a cool-water bath, top off, and remove the candle as you would any other molded candle.

4. You will now have a beautiful chunk candle, but if you are able to take one more step, you

can make the colors in your candle come alive! This step is best done outdoors. Place the candle in a shallow pan. Light a propane torch to a low flame. Pass the flame lightly over the surface of the candle until some of the wax melts away. The idea here is to melt off some of the wax that was poured over the chunks, thereby bringing the color to the surface. Continue on all sides until the desired effect is achieved.

HURRICANE CANDLES

Hurricane candles consist of a votive candle placed inside a translucent wax shell. Thus, no wick is necessary. When the votive candle has burned down, it can be replaced again and again, and your hurricane shell will last a very long time.

Hurricane molds can also be made by creating a shell with a high melting point and pouring wax with a lower melting point into the wax shell (use the wax formulation for container candles on page 47). An example of this type of hurricane appears below.

Hurricanes are best made in metal molds. A diameter of at least 4 inches (10 cm) is required to allow heat to escape properly without melting the shell, but 6 inches (15 cm) or more is preferred. For this reason, special hurricane molds are available.

In spite of their name, hurricanes should not be used in strong draughts; if wind causes the flame of the votive to splay to one side, the heat can damage the inside of the shell. Using paraffin wax with a higher melting point will increase the longevity of the hurricane shell.

Keepsake Candles, Bartlesville, Oklahoma

additional supplies

Paraffin wax, 156° F (69° C) melting point

Micro 170 or micro 180

Metal mold, at least 4 inches (10 cm) in diameter, and preferably 6 inches (15 cm) or more or a special hurricane mold

instructions

1. Select a mold and secure the wick hole with mold sealer if necessary. Prepare a cool-water bath.

2. Melt enough paraffin wax to completely fill

the mold you have chosen. For every 5 pounds (1.8 kg) of paraffin wax you have used, you should add ½ pound (227 g) of microcrystalline wax with a melting point of 170° to 180° F (77° to 82° C). This will make the wax less brittle, harder, and therefore more durable. If microcrystalline waxes are not available, use 100 percent paraffin wax.

3. Melt the microcrystalline waxes in a separate container, add the micro wax to the paraffin wax, and bring the temperature to 190° F (88° C). Pour the wax into the prepared mold. Place the mold in a cool-water bath to the depth of the entire candle.

4. When the wax has hardened to form a shell slightly more than ¼ inch (.5 cm) thick, carefully pour the still liquid wax back into your melting pot. If the shell is less than ¼ inch- (.5 cm) thick, it will be too frail. It is better to err by making the shell too thick. Place the mold on a level surface and allow to cool completely. If excess wax has drizzed inside of the mold, cut if off cleanly with a sharp knife. When the wax is hard, place the mold in the refrigerator for about 15 minutes and carefully remove it from the mold. You are now ready to put a votive candle inside and enjoy the delicate light show.

TIE-DYED CANDLES

These candles remind me of the tie-dyed shirts popular in the 1960s. The swirling colors in the lighter-colored wax have quite an unusual effect and are easy to make.

additional supplies

2 or 3 bold colors of candle dye

Uncolored, off-white, or white wax chunks

Several small cans or jar lids

Small frying pan

Several small metal spoons bent to form ladles

instructions

1. Prepare and wick your mold. Place the uncolored, off-white, or white wax chunks in the mold as you would when making a chunk candle. Prepare the cool-water bath so that the candle will be immersed up to the rim of the mold.

2. Choose two or three colors to use from the dyes you have on hand. For a nice effect, your dyes will need to be bold, not pastel. Also, you will get the best results from colors that are not closely related. Place small cans or jar lids in a small frying pan. Place a small chunk of dye in each and melt it.

3. Melt additional plain, white, or off-white wax in the wax melter. By using uncolored wax, the colors from the dyes will have more of an effect. Carefully bring the temperature of the wax to 275° F (135° C). (This high temperature allows the dyes to travel through the wax easily.) Do not leave the wax unattended while heating it to this high temperature. Pour this wax into the mold.

4. Quickly (but calmly) ladle two or three spoonfuls of colored wax along the inside wall of the mold. Turn the mold 1 or 2 inches (2.5 or 5 cm), and, using a clean ladle and a different color wax, repeat this process. Keep turning the mold until you have gone around the entire edge of the mold. Count or time 40 to 60 seconds and immediately immerse the candle into the cool-water bath to stop the progress of the dye. Top off, cool, and remove just as you would any other molded candles.

seven gifts

In traditional Christian lore, the seven-branched candelabrum is symbolic of the seven gifts of the Holy Spirit: counsel, peace, knowledge, piety, wisdom, strength, and understanding.

INTERIOR DECORATED CANDLES

Interior decorated candles allow you to add texture and design to molded block candles. The decorative material is held in place on the outside of the candle's shell by a sleeve or insert. As the wax hardens, the sleeve is removed; the decorative material stays in place on the candle's outer surface. The effect of interior decorated candles can be heightened by melting off some of the exterior wax with a propane torch. The decorative materials you use are up to you, but natural items such as dried flowers, pine cones, shells, or colorful stones work exceptionally well.

wax formulation

Paraffin wax, 140° F (60° C) melting point

1 tablespoon (15 ml) clear crystals per pound (454 g) of wax (Do not substitute for these as other additives will make the wax more opaque, and lessen the decorative effect.)

additional supplies

Round or oval metal or acrylic mold

Dried flowers, pine cones, seashells, etc. These materials need to be about 1 inch (2.5 cm) wide.

Interior sleeve or length of stainless steel pipe, 1 inch (2.5 cm) smaller in diameter than your mold

Watch or clock for checking the time

Propane torch *

*optional

instructions

1. Prepare and wick the mold as usual, taking care to leave enough wick attached to account

Angel Lady Designs®, Olympia, Washington

for the extra height of the sleeve, if it is taller than your mold.

2. Melt the wax in your wax melter and bring it to the proper temperature for the type of mold you are using (see page 54).

3. Choose the decorative material. Position the sleeve in the candle mold; make certain that it is centered and be sure to pull the wick up through the sleeve.

4. Place the decorative material between the sleeve and the wall of the mold. You may need to use a length of wire to help arrange the material.

5. Prepare the cool-water bath. When the wax is the proper temperature, pour the wax into the center of the sleeve. The wax will fill the outer area of the mold as you fill the mold with wax.

6. Place the mold in the cool-water bath and add water to the height of the candle. Begin timing; after one minute, gently pull up on the sleeve, moving it up in the mold about ½ inch (1.5 cm) or so. It will rest on the wax that has hardened on the bottom of the mold. Begin timing again and repeat this process after another minute has passed. Keep repeating

this process until you can remove the sleeve from the mold completely. At some point, depending on the height of the mold, you will have to place the wick and rod to the side until the sleeve is removed.

7. As the candle cools, top off as for any other molded candle.

Angel Lady Designs®, Olympia, Washington

8. Remove the candle from the mold. If you wish to make the imbedded material more apparent, you may do so by using a propane torch to melt off the exterior wax. You should not be intimidated by the procedure, as it is quite easy to do. Simply place the candle on a shallow tin can that has been placed inside a pan or pie plate to catch the excess wax. Light the torch and move it slowly back and forth over a small area. Soon wax will be melting off the sides of the candle; turn it as you expose the materials and start melting in a new area. This process brings the texture of the material to the surface! Be careful not to burn the material by placing the torch too close to the surface.

VOTIVE CANDLES

These popular molded candles are easy to make. Usually votive molds are sold in groups of six. They are best when made with a special wax formulation, such as the one described below. Because they are so small, votive candles do not require a cool-water bath.

wax formulation

This formula works well for the votive mold I have used for several years. Each candle measures $1\frac{5}{8}$-inch (4.1 cm) high with a $1\frac{1}{2}$-inch (4 cm) diameter. These votives burn well without collapsing at the end, as some votives do. You may find that you will need to alter the formula if the cavities in your mold are radically different in size.

• 90 percent paraffin with a 131° F (55° C) melting point, 6 percent stearic acid, 2 percent microcrystalline wax with a 180° F (82° C) melting point, and 2 percent luster crystals.

wicks

Votive candles require lead- or wire-core wicks. These wicks, with the help of a wick tab, will stand erect until the votive has finished burning. The mold manufacturer's information will indicate the size of lead-core wicking you should use (small, medium, or large). Most votive molds will use small lead-core wick and small wick tabs.

materials

Wax formulation as described above

Lead- or wire-core wicks, enough for 6 votives, plus a few extra inches (5 cm)

Wick tabs

*Candle dye

equipment

Wax melter

Candy thermometer

Votive molds

Wooden spoon

Old metal spoon bent to form a ladle

Freezer paper

Short piece of wire

Mold-release spray*

*optional

instructions

Votives are poured in the same fashion as other molded candles. The only difficulty is pouring into the tiny opening of each cavity in the mold without spilling the wax. For this reason, I like to pour with a large spoon that is bent to a 45-degree angle at the spot between the handle and the spoon to create a makeshift ladle. (Most commercial ladles are too large to use for votives.)

1. Follow the instructions for molded candles (page 54), omitting the cool-water bath. Prepare the mold, using the appropriate wick for your mold (photo 10).

2. Votives should be poured at 190° F (88° C), unless the mold manufacturer recommends otherwise. Bring the wax to the correct temperature; melt the stearic acid, micro wax, and luster crystals separately and add them to the wax. Place the votive mold on a sheet of freezer paper to catch any spills. Carefully ladle the wax into each opening. Fill each cavity to the top. Try to avoid overfilling the mold cavity. Overfilling can make votives very difficult to remove from the mold. Set the extra wax aside.

3. You will need to check the mold regularly for shrinkage of the wax. When the surface of the wax starts to harden, pierce it with a short piece of wire, making sure that you pierce around the wick along its entire length. This prevents air pockets from forming, which often happens. (Votives are prone to developing air pockets because of the extreme heat of the wax and the small size of each cavity in the mold.) When the wax cools and a well develops, reheat the extra wax, pierce the wax again to expose any air pockets, and refill with the extra wax. Repeat this process if necessary.

4. Once the wax has hardened, you can remove the votives from the mold. If your mold is plastic (like mine), the candles will sometimes stick. Mold-release spray will help prevent this from happening. You can also place the mold in the refrigerator for about 20 minutes and the candles should release easily. Trim the wick on top to about ⅜ inch (1 cm). Thread a wick tab onto the wick at the base of each votive, pressing it into the wax. Trim off any excess wick.

hand-dipped tapers

Dipping tapers by hand is perhaps the most ancient form of candlemaking still practiced on a regular basis. Tapers appeal to crafters because the process has an age-old rhythm and because tapers have a wonderful simplicity, both in the finished form and in the materials.

Hand-dipped tapers are made by repeatedly dipping a wick into melted wax. Dipping tapers can take an hour or so; if you are making very long tapers, it can take all afternoon. Longer tapers not only need more time to cool between dips, but the amount of wax needed can take more than an hour to melt. Leave yourself plenty of extra time, especially if you have never dipped tapers before. Usually 30 to 45 dips in the wax are necessary, but the simple elegance of the final product makes hand-dipped tapers well worth the effort.

The most efficient way to dip tapers is to use a cool-water bath or multiple dipping rings. With multiple rings, the first tapers dipped have cooled by the time their next turn comes around.

CHOOSING A WICKING METHOD

There are several ways to arrange the wick for dipped tapers. The method that you choose will depend on your budget, the ease of acquiring supplies, the time you choose to put into the craft, and the items you have on hand.

Using a naked wick is the simplest way to make one pair of tapers. To make more than one pair at a time, you may want to use either a wick holder or a dipping frame; instructions for making both are found in this section, page 75.

Naked wicks. Tapers are always dipped in pairs. The easiest way to make one pair of tapers is to dip a primed naked wick into the wax repeatedly. An extra length of wick loops over your fingers and separates the tapers so they do not rub together and mar the candle surface during the dipping process.

The obvious advantage to this method of wicking is simplicity. However, despite your best efforts, there will still be a tendency for your candles to develop sags or ridges. There are several methods to prevent this from happening. One approach is to weight the wick with a lead sinker or heavy metal washer. Another method is to dip the taper in as hot a wax as possible. Using luster crystals in your wax formula will also minimize sagging (see Wax Formulations on page 78). Placing your dipping vat in a double boiler can also minimize sags and ridges because that set up helps to keep the temperature of the wax more constant. If all else fails and you wind up with lumpy tapers, let the final dips harden slightly and then roll the candles on a clean sheet of freezer paper to smooth the edges. Having said all this, if you desire or are satisfied with a more rustic-looking candle that is not perfectly tapered, you will probably want to dip a naked wick.

Wick holders. Using a wick holder is an easy way to dip more than one pair of tapers at a time. The actual size and shape of your wick holder should be determined by the shape of your dipping vat. A wick holder uses pairs of hooks screwed into a piece of wood to accommodate the wicks and to keep the tapers from rubbing together. Wick holders are easy to use, but tapers made with them may also exhibit a somewhat rough, rustic finish. See the instructions for making a simple wick holder on this page.

Dipping frames. A dipping frame will help you make perfect tapers with smooth sides. A professional dipping frame can accommodate four pairs of tapers. The dipping frame shown is a simplification of the dipping ring used by professional candlemakers. It makes two pairs of tapers at a time, is easy to make, and is inexpensive.

It is well worth the effort to make a couple of these frames if you plan to dip a lot of tapers. This dipping frame is adjustable and will make tapers 3 inches (7.5 cm) to 1 foot (.3 m) long. It is narrow and can be used with narrow dipping vats.

MAKING A WICK HOLDER

A wick holder that can accommodate more than one pair of tapers is practical and easy to use. The wick holder pictured can accommodate three pairs of tapers (photo 1). It is made from the simplest of materials and is easy enough for a child to

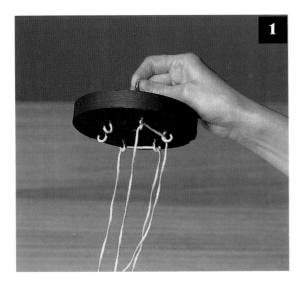

make. It can be used to dip tapers in a 3-pound (1.3 kg) coffee can, or you can modify the plans to size the wick holder to your dipping vat.

materials

1   4½-inch (11.5 cm) round piece of wood, ¾ inch (2 cm) thick
Pencil
1   Small nail
1   Large screw eye
6   ¾-inch (2 cm) screw hooks

instructions

1. Measure ½ inch (1.5 cm) in from the outside edge of the wood and mark it with a pencil all around the perimeter of the wood. Connect these points to create a circle.

2. Choose a starting point on this circle and mark it. From this point, measure 1¾ inches (4.5 cm) and mark it. Continue measuring 1¾ inches (4.5 cm) all around the circle, marking each point as you go. When you are finished, there should be six marks on the circle.

3. Mark each of the hash marks you have made with a dot where the mark and the circle intersect. On each dot, use a nail to start a hole for the screw hooks. Screw a hook into each location.

4. Find and mark the center on top of the wood. Using a nail, start a hole for the screw eye. Attach the screw eye to the wood.

MAKING A DIPPING FRAME

This dipping frame (photo on page 77), made from materials that can be found in any good hardware store, can help you make perfect tapers. Another advantage is that it is adjustable; it will

Bright Lights, Lower Lake, California

dip tapers from 3 to 12 inches (7.5 to 30.5 cm) in length, but is particularly useful for making tapers over 6 inches (15 cm) long.

materials

1   3-foot (.9 m) threaded steel rod, ¼ inch (.5 cm) diameter

4   Nuts to fit the steel rod

4   Lock washers to fit the steel rod

1   Screw-eye bolt, ¼ inch (.5 cm) diameter

1   1½-inch (4 cm) coupling nut to fit the steel rod

2   Stainless-steel sink baskets with drainage holes, with all the hardware removed; these can be new or, better yet, recycled! Check to be sure that the opening in the center is large enough to slip over the steel rod.

equipment

Hacksaw

Metal file

instructions

1.   Using the hacksaw, cut the steel rod in half. File the rough edges with the metal file until smooth.

2.   Screw or thread on the following items 2 inches (5 cm) from the end of the rod (in this order): one nut, one lock washer, one sink basket with the open end down (open end facing away from the longer section of rod), one lock washer, one nut. Tighten the nuts to hold the sink basket firm. This will be the bottom of your dipping frame.

3.   Screw or thread on the following items on the opposite end of the rod (in this order): one nut, one lock washer, one sink basket with the open end up, one lock washer, one nut.

Tighten the nuts to hold the basket firm. This is the top of the dipping frame. By adjusting the location of the top basket on the rod, you can vary the length of the tapers you make.

4.   Screw on the coupling nut partially and tighten it down. Thread on the screw eye as far as it will go. This will be the hanger.

WICKING THE DIPPING FRAME

instructions

1.   Thread the wick through one of the holes on the bottom basket and tie securely.

2.   Thread the wick through the corresponding hole on the top basket. Be sure that the wick is straight. There should be enough play in the baskets to turn them slightly if the holes are not identically aligned. The wick should be as tight as you can manage without straining it. You will have to adjust this tension again before tying and cutting the wick.

3.   Count three holes over and thread the wick throught the fourth hole.

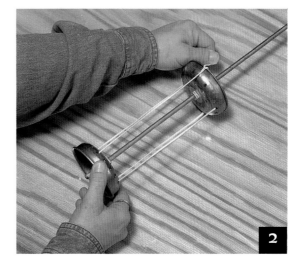

4. Thread the wick through the corresponding hole on the bottom basket. Tie the wick securely, making sure that both wicks stay taut. Cut off the extra wick.

5. Thread the other side of the dipping frame in the same fashion. Before dipping, double-check to be sure that the wick is taut and as straight as possible (photo 2, page 77).

WAX FORMULATIONS

Tapers can be made from several different formulations of wax. The melting point of the paraffin you use is the most important variant; tapers made from wax with an inappropriate melting point will dip excessively and burn poorly. Below are some wax combinations you may wish to try for dipping tapers.

• 100 percent paraffin wax with a 140° to 145° F (60° to 63° C) melting point

• 90° percent paraffin wax with a 140° to 145° F (60° t 63° C) melting point, and 10 percent beeswax

• 100 percent paraffin with a 140° to 145° F (60° to 63° C) melting point, with 5 tablespoons (74 ml) stearic acid and 1 tablespoon (14.8 ml) luster crystals added per pound (454 g) of wax (especially good for dipping with a naked wick)

• 100 percent beeswax

WICK

Flat-braided wicks work best for tapers. For tapers under 1 inch (2.5 cm) in diameter, use 15-ply flat-braided wick. For tapers over 1 inch (2.5 cm) in diameter, use 24-ply flat-braided wick. For tapers made of 100 percent beeswax, use 24-ply flat-braided wick for all sizes.

TEMPERATURE

Tapers can be dipped at temperatures from 160° to 180° F (71° to 82° C). The dipping temperature will affect the finish on the candle. Dipped at 160° F (71° C), the tapers will have a grainy finish and may be lumpy. Dipped at 180° F (82° C), the tapers will have a smooth, glossy finish. Dipping at 170° F (77° C) is prudent and gives a nice finish. If you want a glossy finish, you can raise the temperature of the wax to 180° F (82° C) for the final dip.

A note on dipping long tapers: If the temperature in your dipping vat is 170° F (77° C) near the top of the vat, it is likely to be higher than that at the bottom. Because of the length of the tapers, each dip takes substantially more time than with shorter tapers. If the temperature at the bottom of the vat is over 180° F (82° C), the tapers may lose some wax on each dip and become slightly narrower at the bottom than they should be. To head off this problem, take the temperature of the wax as close to the bottom of the vat as possible and be aware that the problem may develop. Tapers that are narrower at the bottom can be overdipped a few times after they are taken off the dipping ring to correct the problem.

MAKING DIPPED TAPERS

The following lists detail the items you will need for dipping tapers.

materials

Paraffin wax, melting point of 140° to 145° F (60° to 63° C)

Beeswax*

Stearic acid*

Luster crystals*

Flat-braided wick, 15- or 24-ply

Candle dye and fragrance*

equipment

Large pan for the bottom of the double boiler

Dipping vat

Candy thermometer

Cool-water bath*

Wick holder*

Dipping frame *

Hooks or place to hang the candles between dips*

*optional

instructions

Having the working order of dipping candles firmly established in your mind can keep you from doing quite a bit of fumbling on candlemaking day! The setup and technique listed below have worked well for me.

1. Setting up your dipping vat: Choose the pot you will be using as a bottom for your double-boiler setup. If your tapers are short enough, it is easier (as we have done here) to use a wax melter as the dipping vat. Place the dipping vat in the pan and put it on the stove top. Place wax chunks in the dipping vat about as deep as the tapers you are making are long. Keep track of the weight of the wax if you are using a wax formula that uses additives.

   NOTE: Under certain circumstances, tapers dipped in a wax melter without a double-boiler pot underneath it can develop sags or ridges. This occurs because of uneven temperatures of the wax in the melter or because the temperature of the wax fluctuates too quickly.

If you experience this, you may want to use a double-boiler setup.

2. Melting the wax: Slowly add water to the pan, making sure not to tip the dipping vat. Ideally the water should come up at least one-half the height of the dipping vat, more if you can do so without tipping it over or causing it to float. Place the vat on a burner over medium heat; you do not want the water to boil wildly, but want it just hot enough to melt the wax and bring it to the right temperature. When some of the wax begins to melt, place a candy thermometer in the liquid wax.

3. Preparing the wicks: This will vary, depending on the method you are using. If you are dipping naked wicks or are using a wick holder, the wicks will be much easier to work with if they are primed at this point (see page 19). If you are using a dipping frame, priming is not necessary, so follow the directions on page 77 for threading the dipping frame.

4. Adjusting the level of the wax: Check on the melting wax. It is likely that you will need to add more wax to the dipping vat at this point. The main factor in the depth of the wax is the length of the tapers you are making, so gently add more wax if necessary. NOTE: Wax expands slightly as it is heated, so you are better off adding it a little at a time.

5. Set up a cool-water bath: If you are using a cool-water bath to speed up the dipping process, set it up now. Be certain that the cool-water bath is able to accommodate the entire length of the taper. Place the cool-water bath in a nearby location, perhaps on an empty burner on the stove top.

6. Final adjustment of the additives and wax temperature: If you are using additives in your tapers, they should be stirred in now. Remember that additives with high melting points such as luster crystals should be melted separately first, then added to the wax. To do this, use a small tin can; add the correct amount of additives in proportion to the number of pounds of wax you have melted (see page 21) and melt them over hot water on a spare burner. Stir into the wax thoroughly. Check the temperature of the wax. When the temperature reaches 170° F (77° C), turn the burner down to keep the temperature steady. You are ready to begin dipping!

7. Dipping procedure: Dip the wicks into the liquid wax for three or four seconds, then remove the wicks from the wax. If you are using the dipping ring, allow the excess wax to drain off (photo 3). You can give the ring a shake, but do not tip it. Wait until the excess wax has drained off, then hang the wicks or dip them momentarily into the cool-water bath.

If you are using the cool-water bath, you must be sure to allow all the water to drain off the taper before dipping again or bubbles will form on the surface. If you are using the wick holder or naked wicks, take care that the tapers do not swing back and forth and touch each other during the dipping and hanging process.

If you are not using the cool-water bath, let the wax harden on the wicks for two minutes or so before dipping again. Continue dipping the wicks into the liquid wax. It usually takes 30 to 40 dips to achieve complete tapers. Check the temperature periodically to be sure that it does not deviate too much.

After you have dipped awhile, you may need to replace some of the wax, especially if you are making long tapers. Always replace the wax slowly. Take into account that when you dip the tapers again, they will displace some of the wax. If you add too much wax in the dipping vat, liquid wax will spill over the edge and seep into the water bath. Continue dipping until the tapers are the desired size (photo 4).

8. Final step: To give the tapers a smooth, glossy finish, heat the wax to 180° F (82° C) and give them a final dip (photo 5). Hang the tapers up to cool for about 10 minutes. Trim the ends with a sharp knife or a pair of sharp scissors (photo 6).

FINISHING TOUCHES
making perfect ends

If you plan to use the tapers in candlesticks or other holders, the ends can be finished with a base former. Place the base former in an old frying pan and heat it on a moderate setting on the stove. When thoroughly heated, place the end of each taper in the base former for just a few seconds, then remove them (photo 7). The excess wax will be caught in the frying pan, and you will have perfectly made taper ends!

color

The best way to give color to tapers is through a process called *overdipping*. Overdipped candles are made from uncolored wax first, then dipped several times in colored wax. By overdipping, you eliminate the need to color the large amount of wax in which you dip; this wax can then be used for other purposes. Tapers can also be given a marbleized look by overdipping them in a certain fashion. For complete instructions on overdipping techniques, refer to the section on specialty candles, page 84.

Susan Schadt Designs, Del Mar, California

PREVENTING WARM WEATHER SAG

Many of us who live in hot climates have had tapers that have "swooned" in very hot weather. There is a way to prevent this when making your own tapers. As you are finishing the dipping process, prepare a dipping vat to hold a small amount of paraffin with a melting point of 180° F (82° C). Melt the wax and overdip the tapers quickly. Lingering too long at this temperature will melt away the tapers you have worked so hard to create! If you cannot find paraffin with a 180° F (82° C) melting point, a combination of luster crystals with a melting point of 190° F (88° C) and paraffin with a melting point of 140° to 145° F (60° to 63° C) may be substituted. Mix 1 ounce (28 g) paraffin to every 2 ounces (56 g) of luster crystals used.

SPIRALED TAPERS

Spiraled tapers are surprisingly easy to make once you have a few practice runs under your belt. While the tapers are still quite warm, spread them out on a clean sheet of waxed paper. Using a large, clean dowel or rolling pin, gently begin to flatten the taper about 1 inch (2.5 cm) above the base. Gently roll the dowel up the taper until you are almost—but not quite—at the tip. Pick the taper up and gently and slowly twist the taper with your fingertips. Take care to keep the twists as evenly spaced as possible.

Continue to twist the taper all the way to the top. If the taper cracks during this process, it was not warm enough. The tapers can always be warmed by placing them back in the dipping vat

for a few seconds. Tapers with smaller diameters will cool much faster than larger tapers and need to be twisted more quickly.

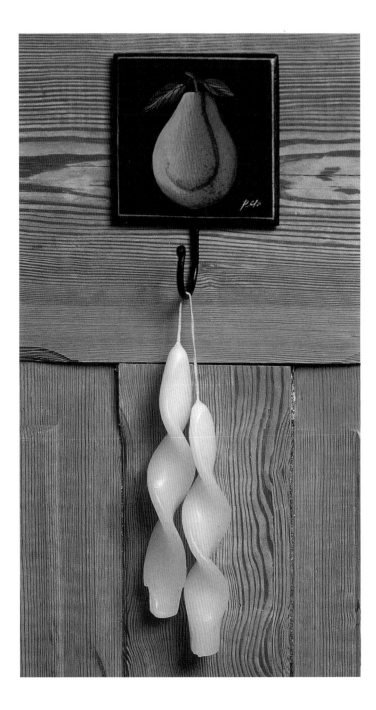

specialty candles

Let There Be Light, Asheville, North Carolina.

Specialty candles are candles that have a distinct look or are made using a special technique. Some of the candles in this section, such as rolled beeswax candles, are easy enough for children to make. However, rolled spiral candles and sand candles require some practice and considerable concentration. For others, such as water candles, you will need a special wax formulation in order to procure the best results.

You should not be afraid to try to make some of the more difficult specialty candles. You probably will have to try a certain technique several times before you acquire the necessary skill to make a candle you are satisfied with, but the result is well worth the effort and you will feel a keen sense of accomplishment when you master the new technique! Any special equipment needed to make the candles will be listed at the beginning of each candle's instructions.

ROLLED BEESWAX TAPERS

Rolled beeswax candles are very simple to make and have an elegant and classic look. They are made from preformed wax sheets that are imprinted with the honeycomb design that appears on natural beeswax. The sheets are available in either the natural beeswax color or assorted colors.

For economy, plan the size and shape of your candles in advance. Two medium block candles or two tapered pillar candles can be cut from one sheet by cutting the sheet in half either lengthwise or diagonally. You can also make one large pillar candle from a sheet of beeswax.

materials

Clean beeswax sheets

Wick: Rolled beeswax candles under 2 inches (5 cm) in diameter use #2 or #3 square-braided wick; rolled beeswax candles over 2 inches (5 cm) in diameter use #5 or #6 square-braided wick

Patti Hill, Weaverville, North Carolina

equipment

Craft knife

Clean cookie sheet or freezer paper

Hair dryer*

*optional

instructions

1. If you are making a rolled block candle (without tapered edges), cut the wax sheet in half or to the desired height of the candle (photo 1). If you are making a tapered pillar candle, cut the wax diagonally.

2. Place the beeswax on a clean cookie sheet or freezer paper. Warm the wax by placing it in a warm oven very briefly or by using a hair dryer held about 10 inches (25.5 cm) away from the wax. This will warm the wax and prevent it from cracking or breaking as you roll it.

3. Cut the wick to the correct length, leaving enough wick on top to light and about 1 inch (2.5 cm) extra on the bottom. Place the wick on the warm wax along the longest edge (photo 2). Push the wick into the wax to help keep it in place as you roll.

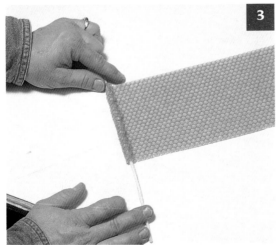

Let There Be Light, Asheville, North Carolina

4. Starting on the edge with the wick, begin to roll the wax. Keep the wax rolled as tightly as you can; a loosely rolled candle will not burn well and may unravel. Roll the wax over the wick, keeping the roll tight without breaking the wax (photo 3).

5. Continue to roll the wax sheet (photo 4). If the wax becomes brittle at any point, warm it up again slightly in the oven or with a hair dryer. When you come to the end of the candle, warm the wax slightly and press the edge into the candle to secure it.

HAND-ROLLED SPIRAL CANDLES AND TAPERS WITH FLARED EDGES

These elegant candles are another type of rolled candle. Making this candle is not as easy as using beeswax sheets because you must make your own sheet of wax and roll it while the wax is still warm. Microcrystalline wax additive helps make the wax more workable.

Although making these candles is challenging, you will be delighted with the effect of the flared edges. It may take several trial runs before you learn to handle the wax correctly, but it is a skill that can be used when making other types of candles.

materials

Wax formulation: 1 pound (454 g) paraffin wax, 130° F (54° C) melting point (140° F [60° C] can be substituted); 2 ounces (62 g) microcrystalline white beads (to make wax more workable)

Wick: #2 square-braided wick for candles 2 to 3 inches (5 to 7.5 cm) in diameter

equipment

Wax melter

Candy thermometer

Wooden spoon

Clean sheet of freezer paper about 2 feet (.6 m) long or a cookie sheet

Sharp kitchen knife

Non-stick aerosol vegetable oil spray

instructions

1. Microcrystalline wax additive used at 10 percent of the weight of the wax works well. Melt the microcrystalline wax additive in your wax melter. Add the paraffin wax and continue melting.

2. Spray the freezer paper or cookie sheet with vegetable oil and place it on a flat, level surface. If the surface is not level, the wax will be uneven and difficult to roll.

3. When the wax has melted, pour it onto the freezer paper (cut into a rectangle with the edges turned up) or cookie sheet in a layer a little more than ⅛ inch (.3 cm) thick (photo 5). Allow the wax to harden for six to seven minutes. In order to roll the wax, it must not be too warm or too cold. (The wax will stay flexible longer than you think.) When you experience difficulty working with the wax, it is usually because it is too warm.

flared taper

4. Pour the wax and let it harden as described in step 3. Cut it diagonally across the rectangle. Slip the knife blade under the part of the wax you will not be using and start to roll the wax. If it flakes off or if your hand mars the wax and it breaks, it is still too warm to work with. When the wax is the right temperature, slip the knife blade under the piece you will be rolling to loosen it from the freezer paper.

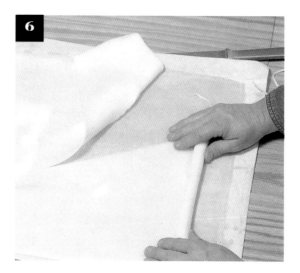

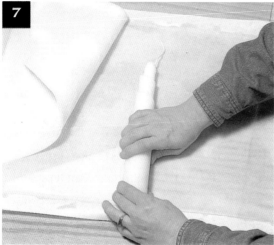

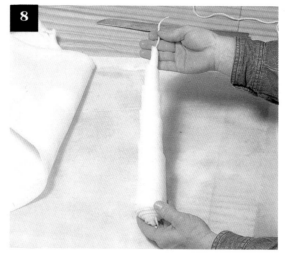

5. Cut enough wick for the candle plus 2 or 3 inches (5 or 7.5 cm). Place the wick along the long edge of the wax and roll the wax around it (photo 6, page 89). Roll the wax as tightly as you can without breaking it. Continue rolling until the entire length of the wax is used (photos 7 and 8, page 89). Secure the end by gently pressing it into the candle. If this does not hold it, attach it with a small amount of melted wax.

6. Cut the bottom edge of the candle off to form an even bottom, leaving the extra wick intact. At this point, the wax should still be flexible. Holding the candle in one hand and running your finger down the cut edge of the candle, gently bend the edge outward to form a flare. You will have to do this a couple of times to get the flared edge to stand away from the surface of the candle for the desired effect. If the edge of the wax cracks, continue working; it can be mended later by heating it a little and adjusting it with your finger.

7. After the candle is formed, it will still be pliable and can be misshapen if it is allowed to cool on its side. To cool the candle, stand it up in a container on its end or hang it securely from the extra wick on the bottom. Should the candle be slightly warped after it cools, see page 44 for information on how to perfect its shape.

   NOTE: For an interesting effect, colored wax can be marbled through the wax immediately after it has been poured onto the baking sheet. Simply use a knife to swirl the colored wax through the uncolored wax.

WATER CANDLES

Water candles are among my favorite candles to make—each is a unique piece of candle art. They require quite a bit of effort, but like a hurricane candle, they will last a very long time because the water candle portion is never really burned.

Water candles require the addition of a small amount of microcrystalline wax to the wax formulation. They are quite a bit more difficult to accomplish without this additive. For best results, water candles should be worked in a 32-gallon (144 l) trash can (the larger the opening, the better) or in a large metal or plastic tub.

materials

A finished candle—either a sturdy pillar candle or a block candle, at least 4 to 5 inches (10 to 12.5 cm) tall.

Wax formulation: 6½ pounds (2.4 kg) of paraffin wax, 140° F (60° C) melting point and 11 ounces (341 g) micro wax to make the wax more workable

equipment

Wax melter

Wooden spoon

32-gallon (144 l) trash can or large set tub filled to within 8 inches (20.5 cm) of the rim with cold water (this vessel should be at least 2 feet [.6 m] deep and very clean)

Disposable pie plate

instructions

1. Melt the micro wax in your wax melter. Add the paraffin wax and heat to 170° F (77° C). Pour the wax mixture into the pie plate, centering the block or pillar candle in the middle (photo 9, page 92). Harden the wax by placing the pie plate in the cold water in the trash can (photo 10, page 92). When the wax has

hardened, separate the candle—now firmly anchored in the wax—from the pie plate.

2. Make sure the wax is still at 170° F (77° C). If you are working in a trash can, you will need a place to sit (for comfort) and a place to rest the wax melter (for safety). Sitting beside the trash can, hold the top of the candle and position one side of the base of the wax at about a 45-degree angle with the water.

3. Pour the wax onto the rim (photo 11). A small pool will form. Gently and slowly thrust the rim deep into the water, twisting it as you go (photo 12). The slower you go, the more substantial and stronger the wax will be. The wax will harden in a display of wispy shapes. Continue pouring wax and pushing it into the water until you achieve a pleasing shape.

4. Turn the rim around a few inches and begin pouring again, this time adjacent to the first area of hardened wax. Keep turning and pouring until you are pleased with the results (photos 13 through 16). Light the block or

pillar candle and enjoy the way the light plays off the sculptured wax around it. Replace the candle as necessary.

5. You will no doubt have wax bubbles floating in the water when your candle is finished. It is possible to reuse them, but you must do it carefully! These wax bubbles contain water and, if they are heated, the water can spurt out of the hot wax, burning you seriously or hitting you in the face.

To reuse this wax, do the following: Fish out the wax bubbles with a tea strainer or colander. Place them in a shallow layer on a tray and allow them to dry for several days or until the surface is completely dry. Roll over them with a rolling pin or similar object, breaking the wax into small crumbs. (Water will be released from pockets of wax that have surrounded it.) Dry the wax thoroughly in a warm place. If any pieces remain that cannot be treated in this fashion, throw them away. Do not reuse them!

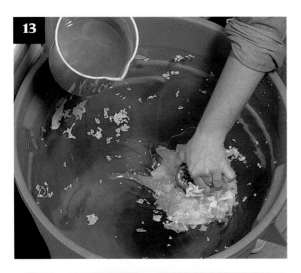

SAND CANDLES

When you are making sand candles, the pouring temperature of the wax is critical. Pouring temperature can make all the difference in how the finished candle looks. If the pouring temperature is low (155° F or 68° C), the surface of the final candle will not attach to the sand. If the temperature is high (250° to 300° F or 121° to 149° C), the surface will be encrusted with sand. This is useful to understand, because if you ever need to make a candle in a certain shape, but lack a mold, you can always try to improvise with a sand candle poured at a low temperature.

If you desire the sand-laden look, you must be extremely careful when heating the wax to these high temperatures! The flash point of the paraffin wax formulation in the instructions is roughly 400° F (204° C), and as the temperature goes above 250° F (121° C), much caution must be exercised, just as if you were heating oil on the stove.

Other variables such as the type and consistency of sand you choose will affect the look of your finished candle. Colored terrarium sand could be used if you wish to go to the added expense. The moisture content of the sand also influences the outcome. Dry sand is easier for the wax to penetrate, but it is difficult to get it to hold a shape. Therefore, to help build up a nice layer of sand on the surface, make your form in damp sand, allow it to dry out for several days, then pour the candle.

materials

Sand: any sand that is free of dirt and debris

An object for making the impression in the sand, such as a bowl or a square block of wood

Old sand candle*

Small jar lid: used in the bottom of the candle to keep the bottom from burning out and creating a fire hazard

Wax formulation: 50 percent paraffin wax, 145° F (63° C) melting point; 50 percent paraffin wax, 156° F (69° C) melting point; 12 percent of the combined weight of the micro 180

Candle dye*

High-quality aerosol lacquer or varnish spray*

Wick: heavy wire-core wicking

equipment

A pit to hold the sand: a dishpan works well and is portable, making it unnecessary for you to walk to the sand pit with hot wax

Sprinkling can

Wax melter

Candy thermometer

Length of wire or an awl

Soft paintbrush

Propane torch*

Drill with ¼-inch (1 cm) drill bit

Awl

*optional

instructions

1. Place the sand in a dishpan or similar container. Dampen the sand with a sprinkling can. Do not get the sand any wetter than you have to; it should be only damp enough to hold the shape of the depression. If you can allow the depression to dry out for several days, the wax will penetrate the sand much better and you will have a crusty coating of sand on the outside of the candle.

2. Make the depression in the sand. Take care to firm up the sand on all sides of the object you

use to make the depression, leaving no loose sand or air pockets. If you have an old, nicely shaped sand candle with legs, it will be easier to make your depression from it than it will be to dig it out and make legs yourself. If you must form legs freehand, try to get them as even as possible so the candle will not wobble.

3. Place the jar lid in the depression (photo 17). It should be centered under the spot where the wick will be. If you are using multiple wicks, depending on their placement and the size of the candle, you may need to have more than one lid. (The jar lid is a safety precaution to prevent the bottom of the candle from burning through and possibly starting a fire.)

4. Heat the wax to the desired temperature. The sand candles should be poured white because a high pouring temperature distorts the color of the dye. The dye should be added only to the last layer.

If you substitute another wax formulation, do not heat the wax above 225° F (107° C). You should never leave wax unattended on the stove, but if you are heating wax to a very high temperature for a sand candle, this safety rule becomes doubly important. The wax can accelerate in temperature very quickly. Always have a lid close by that will completely cover the wax melter. If the wax should ever catch on fire, turn off the heat, remove the melter from the heat source (if possible), put the lid on tight, and allow the wax to cool.

5. Pour the wax carefully into the jar lid in the depression (photo 18). This will keep the wax from making a hole in the bottom of your sand mold. The more moisture the sand holds, the more noise the wax will make when it is poured. You should expect a lot of bubbling and crackling as you pour.

6. Allow the wax to cool and skim over. Your candle will have shrunk about ½ inch into the depression. Reheat the remaining wax on the stove to 200° F (93° C). Add the desired dye color to the wax. Pour the dyed wax to fill the remaining depression in the sand (photo 19, page 96).

7. When the candle has hardened, remove it carefully from the sand. Brush off any excess sand with a soft brush or a spray from the garden hose. Choose one of the finishing techniques below to give the candle a smoother finish and to keep it from shedding sand. Allow the candle to dry completely before using one of the finishing techniques.

    Technique #1: Spray the sand-covered portion of the candle with a high-quality aerosol lacquer or varnish. Do not spray the surface of the wax or the wick.

    Technique #2: Run a low flame from a propane torch back and forth over the outside of the candle in an even, sweeping motion. Do not allow any sand and wax to melt off. You should be able to see the sand change color, an indication that the surface has been sealed.

8. Wick insertion: To position the wick or wicks in your sand candle you will need a drill and drill bit that is slightly larger than the wick itself. Choose the placement of the wick (s) and mark it lightly with the tip of an awl or other sharp object. Warm the drill bit in hot water and drill slowly until you hit—but do not pierce—the jar lid (photo 20). A primed wick will be easier to push into the wax because of the added stiffness. Insert the wick in the hole all the way to the lid (photo 21). If you have difficulty pushing the wick through, enlarge the hole by drilling with a slightly larger drill bit or by inserting the hot tip of an awl in the hole to melt away some of the wax. Trim the top of the wick to ½ inch (1.5 cm).

notes on decorating sand candles

Once you have learned the basic technique for making sand candles, it is fun to try decorating them. To achieve textured results, you can place stones, either plain or colored, along the sides of the depression. They will be incorporated in the surface after the candle has hardened. You can use shells or any other nonflammable objects in the same manner.

Sand candles can also be mounted on driftwood and are quite attractive when displayed in this way. The driftwood is placed strategically in or adjacent to the depression to be included in the candle when the wax is poured. The candle may rest on the driftwood or the driftwood may act as a background piece or even a mechanism to mount the candle on the wall (if it is strong enough to hold the weight of the candle).

FLOATING CANDLES

Floating candles are very simple to make and are cast in small, shallow molds made specially for them. Several of these candles floating in a pretty bowl with flowers makes a wonderful table centerpiece for any occasion.

You may find pretty molds for floating candles among candy molds or tart pans. The mold itself needs no wick hole, because the wick is inserted

Sue Teckow, Asheville, North Carolina

after the wax has hardened. Floating candles look beautiful when no additives are used in the wax and when they are colored slightly to retain as translucent a look as possible.

materials

Wax formulation: Paraffin wax, 140° F (60° C) melting point

Wick: Small wire- or lead-core wick

Equipment

Wax melter

Candy thermometer

Floating candle molds, improvised or purchased

Freezer paper

Large bowl

Tapestry needle

Sharp knife

instructions

1. Melt the wax to 165° F (74° C).

2. Lay the floating candle molds out on a sheet of freezer paper; this will catch any wax that drips while you are pouring into the tiny molds. Because the molds harden quickly, you may wish to make floating molds assembly-line style; it is efficient to make a large number from the same wax and then wick them all at once.

3. Prime a length of wire-core wick (see page 19). The wick will be cut to the appropriate length for the molds you have chosen after all the candles are made.

4. Pour the wax into the molds and allow the wax to harden.

5. Place all the candles on the freezer paper. Bring some water to a boil and pour the boil-

ing water into a bowl. Keep this bowl to the side as you work on placing the wick in each candle, reheating the water when necessary.

6. Dip the tapestry needle into the hot water long enough to warm it. Pierce the center of each candle with the tapestry needle all the way through to the back. The hole should be a clean one, small enough for the wick to slip through easily, but not so large that the wick will slide out.

7. When all the candles have wick holes, cut wicks to the correct length, making sure that you have a little extra wick to work with. Insert the wick into each hole, drawing it through the back of the candle a bit. Trim the wick to the correct length on the top of the candle and trim the wick flush with the back of the candle. Turn the candles over, with the tops facing down, and put a couple of wax droplets from a lit candle on the wick hole to seal each candle and to keep the wick from absorbing water.

CUT TAPERS AND CUT-AND-CURL TAPERS

These cut candles have an elegant look and are worth the trouble it takes to make them. Both types of candles are made using the same technique, wax, and instructions. The cut-and-curl tapers are a bit trickier, but once you start to cut the wax, the urge to curl it down the candle is irresistible! This technique can be done on block candles but it is much more difficult to accomplish.

Although this technique may seem advanced, you should not hesitate to try your hand at it. The biggest challenge is developing the correct touch and getting to know the limitations of the wax. It will take a lot of practice to get the curls even each time. The sculpture wax in the wax formulation has many virtues—it helps build layers of wax faster, adds to the tackiness of the wax when it is warm (so the curled strips of wax will stick back on the candle), and hardens the wax once it is cooled, making the curls less frail.

To learn these techniques, you should set aside some candles to practice on; they can always be burned when you are finished— even if they are not perfect!

materials

1 pair of white tapers

Wax formulation: Paraffin wax, 145° F (60° C) melting point and 5 percent (by weight) micro tacky wax

NOTE: The wax will be divided into two colors— one dyed a strong primary color and the other dyed white. Each color should be sufficient in

Crafted by Kaeran Dykes and staff, Dollywood, Pigeon Forge,

quantity to dip the entire length of the tapers you have chosen. The white dye is necessary to show the contrast between the layers of wax. Without the white dye, the uncolored layer will look drab and gray.

White candle dye

Colored candle dye

equipment

Wax melter

Candy thermometer

Wooden spoon

Sharp paring knife

2 cans deep enough to accommodate dipping the tapers or block candle

Pot large enough to hold these cans

Large container for cool-water bath

instructions

1. Heat the micro wax in the wax melter, then add the paraffin wax and continue melting.

2. Plan the pattern you will cut or curl in advance. When the candle is ready to cut or curl, time will be at a premium!

3. Prepare two cans—one to hold the white wax and one to hold the colored wax. Each can should be deep enough to accommodate the tapers you are dipping.

4. Select a pot wide enough to accommodate both cans and place them in it. Partially fill the pot with water and heat it on the stove to just below a boil. Bring the melting wax to 170° F (77° C). Pour half the wax into each can and place the cans in the hot water. Add the white dye to one can and the colored dye

to the other can. Stir until all the dye is melted, adding more, if necessary, to achieve the desired color. Select a can or container to hold a cool-water bath that is deep enough to dip the tapers in.

5. Dip the tapers in the colored wax for about 45 seconds to soften them. Then dip them into the cool-water bath. Remove any water droplets by running your hand or a soft cloth over the taper. (Drops of water on the candle will cause a bubble if the candle is dipped in wax again.)

6. Dip the tapers again into the colored wax, leaving them for only about a second. Return them to the cool-water bath and remove excess water. Repeat this process for a total of about five dips into the colored wax. How many times you will actually dip depends on how fast the wax builds up. You will be able to judge by the intensity of the color.

7. Repeat the dipping/cool-water bath process, this time dipping into the white wax for a total of five dips. Hang the tapers in a secure position at a comfortable height.

8. You are now ready to cut. You have about five minutes in which to work. By now, you should have a pattern in mind and need to concentrate on executing it. General instructions for each technique follow.

Cutting: When you cut tapers, you take a slice off the candle to expose the colored layers beneath the surface. Cut areas should not be too deep or they will weaken the candle as it burns down to them. Slices made by cutting should be evenly spaced around the candle and should be evenly shaped; this comes with practice. Hold the knife firmly in your hand and take a nice even slice off the candle, using a sweeping motion of the wrist. The slice of wax will come completely off the candle. Four slices around a taper are about as many as you can take. Continue taking slices off the taper until a pattern has been formed.

Cut-and-curl candles: Cut-and-curl candles are achieved in the same way as cutting. The difference is that, in cut-and-curl candles, the slice of wax is left attached to the candle. It is then flared backward and reattached to the candle or spiraled like a ringlet and reattached to the candle.

Flared-back cut-and-curl candles: Holding the knife firmly, take a short slice off the candle about 2 inches (5 cm) long; do not complete the slice at the lower end, but leave the wax attached at the bottom. Put the knife down and take hold of the wax strip with your fingers. Flare the wax back to expose the inner surface, then reattach the wax strip to the candle surface by applying light pressure with your finger.

Cut-and-curl spiral candles: Holding the knife firmly, take a slice off the candle about 4 inches (10 cm) long, but leave the wax attached at the bottom. Gently and evenly, spiral the wax all the way to the upper tip, then adhere this slice onto the candle surface by applying pressure with your finger.

special effects

Pictured in the photo above are some of the materials and tools used to create special effects.

This section describes some simple procedures that can be used to alter or enhance the appearance of candles. Some of these procedures require a few simple tools or an extra skill, but many of them are accomplished with everyday household items and are very easy to do. With some practice, you can learn to enhance your homemade candles so that no two ever look alike! For easy reference, these special effects are grouped according to the general technique used—painting techniques, for example.

OVERDIPPED CANDLES

Overdipping is a widely used technique that some candle artisans swear by to give their candles an extra glow when they burn. The process is a simple one: white candles are dipped several times in colored wax as a finishing technique. Overdipping can also be used to give unique color patterns to candles, such as shaded colors and marbled candles.

OVERDIPPING SOLID COLORS

materials

Paraffin wax, 140° F (60° C) melting point

Colored wax

White tapers

equipment

Large pot

Wooden spoon

instructions

1. Melt the uncolored wax in a vessel deep enough to dip your candle. Melt the dye and

Pictured here are candles that feature many of the special effects described in this section. Foreground: color-graded; left to right: marbleized, stippled, embossed, carved, sponged, and rolled appliqué.

add it to the melted wax until the desired shade is achieved.

2. Holding the candle by the wick, dip the candle into the wax for just a few seconds. Allow extra wax to drip back into the heated wax. Repeat this process until the candle has taken on enough color. It will usually take ten or so dips to give an even, vibrant color.

COLOR-GRADED CANDLES

Color-graded candles have a very old-fashioned look and work best when a strong color is used.

materials

Paraffin wax, 140° F (60° C) melting point

Colored wax

White tapers

equipment

Large pot

Wooden spoon

instructions

1. Melt the wax in a vessel deep enough to dip the desired candle. Melt dye in the color you want to work with and stir it into the melted wax.

2. Dip the candle, submerging the entire length in the colored wax (photo 1). Allow any excess wax to drip off (photo 2). Dip the candle again, this time submerging it only 75 percent of the way into the wax and again allowing excess wax to drip off (photo 3). Submerge the candle again, this time only 50 percent of the way into the wax and allow excess wax to drip off. Then give the candle a final dip, submerging it only 25 percent of the way into the wax.

MARBLEIZED CANDLES

materials

Melted paraffin wax—white or colored

Colored wax

White or colored candle

equipment

Large pot

Toothpick or thin stick

instructions

1. Fill a vessel with water—deep enough to accommodate the desired candle—and heat the water to just under a boil. If the candle is white: Place a small amount of wax that has been dyed white on the surface of the water. Next, place a small amount of wax that has been dyed a color on the surface of the water. With a toothpick or similar object, gently swirl the waxes to form a swirled pattern on the top of the water. Avoid stirring the two colors together. If the candle is colored, follow the instructions above, omitting the white wax.

2. Hold the candle by the wick, and dip it into the colored wax, swirling it as you submerge it. Remove the candle in the same fashion. Repeat if necessary until you achieve the desired effect.

PAINTING TECHNIQUES

For an experienced tole painter, painting candles offers a huge array of decorative possibilities, but painting can also be effectively executed by a novice. The painting techniques listed here are quite simple. Once you get used to the feel of a brush and paint, don't be afraid to improvise and try your hand at free-style painting.

It is a good idea to practice your painting skills on a piece of paper before you take on a candle. Acrylic paints are available in convenient 2-ounce (56 g) containers. They work well on candles, clean up with water, and dry quickly. A jar each of white paint, black paint, and a selection of primary colors is all you need. On a small dish or tray, you can mix almost any color you want, then use the white and black paints to lighten or darken the color.

SPONGING

Sponging is an effective way to soften the look of a darker candle and provide textural interest to plain candles.

materials

Acrylic paints

Natural sea sponge

Paraffin or beeswax candle

equipment

Small tray or dish

instructions

1. Place or mix the paint on the tray. Dampen the sea sponge. Stretch the edge of the sponge that faces away from you to expose the tiny holes in the surface.

2. Dip the sponge lightly in the paint. Blot off excess paint and lightly dab the candle surface (photo 4, page 105). Change the direction of the sponge often to vary the effect. Dip more paint on the sponge only when absolutely necessary.

3. Sponge about half the candle surface, allow the paint to dry, and continue sponging until the entire surface is covered.

STENCILING

Small stencils are attractive candle decorations. Stenciled initials are a great way to personalize a gift of handmade candles—or you can choose a purely decorative stencil.

materials

Stencil of your choice

Candle

Masking tape

Acrylic paints

Spray sealer*

equipment

Scissors

Masking tape

Sponge or stencil brush

Small tray or dish

*optional

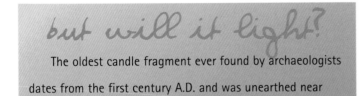

but will it light?

The oldest candle fragment ever found by archaeologists dates from the first century A.D. and was unearthed near Avignon, France.

instructions

1. Choose a stencil that appeals to you and one that will be a good size for your candle—not overwhelmingly large and not so small that it gets lost. Cut the stencil to fit the candle.

2. Tape the stencil securely to the candle in the position where you want it. Make sure the stencil remains snug and will not pull away from the candle.

3. Place a small amount of paint on a tray. Dampen your brush or sponge, then dip the brush or sponge in the paint and blot off any excess paint on the tray.

4. Apply paint with a brush or sponge, blotting inside the stencil opening. Always blot the paint on, do not smudge or try to spread out the paint. Make sure that all the corners and crevices of the stencil are filled with paint. (It is all right to get paint on the stencil itself.)

5. Allow the paint to dry partially and carefully remove the stencil from the candle, taking care not to smudge any of the edges of the paint. Allow the paint to dry. You may wish to spray the stenciled area with an aerosol surface sealer to help protect the painted surface.

FREE-HAND PAINTING

Free-hand painting will not appeal to everyone; not all of us have the ability or the experience to do it well. There are a few things that anyone can do, however. With a little practice, you can make swirled lines or geometric patterns well enough to add some pizazz to a candle. I encourage you to try it!

STIPPLING

Stippling with a brush is another easy painting technique. This looks especially elegant when done in black, navy, silver, gold, or bronze paint over rich, vibrantly colored wax.

materials

Paraffin or beeswax candle

Acrylic paints

equipment

Small, round-point paintbrush

Small dish or tray

instructions

1. Hold the candle firmly, bracing it against your body if necessary. Place the paint in a tray. Dampen the paintbrush.

2. Dip just the point of the brush into the paint, keeping the brush at a 45-degree angle with the paint. At the same angle, place small dots of paint on the candle surface (photo 5). Keep the dots very close together and reapply paint to the brush when necessary.

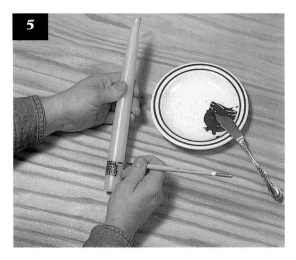

Susan Schadt Designs, Del Mar, California

3. Do a small section of the candle, allow the paint to dry, and continue until the entire candle surface or a portion of it has been painted.

SURFACE ALTERATION

There are many ways to enhance the surface of a candle to create a more interesting appearance. Leather-working tools or ball peen hammers are tools that I have found particularly useful, but the possibilities are endless—use your imagination and look around the house! Embossing tools are also commonly sold through candlemaking suppliers.

For the instructions that follow, use the rounded end of a ball peen hammer, leather-working tools, or any similar piece of equipment.

Two's Company, Mount Vernon, New York

materials

Paraffin or beeswax candle

Towel

equipment

Ball peen hammer

Leather-working tools or similar items

Hammer or mallet

instructions

1. Place the candle on a hard surface with a towel under it. Hold the candle securely in place.

2. Position the tool you have chosen on the surface of the wax. Hit the back or handle of the tool with a hammer or mallet, with just enough force that the blow drives the tool forward into the wax, but not so hard that the candle breaks! This will leave an impression in the wax. If you are using small tools such as leather-working tools, it may be helpful to warm the end several times as you work your way around the candle.

3. Continue striking the candle in this fashion, turning the candle as you go, until the entire surface or a portion of it has been worked (photo 6).

EMBOSSING

Embossing tools have very sharp edges to cut into the candle surface. They are easier to use on a flat or square candle than on a round one. The edge of this tool leaves very fine lines imbedded in the surface of the candle, and each side of the tool features different size teeth.

material

Paraffin or beeswax candle

equipment

Embossing tool

instructions

1. Warm the embossing tool.
2. Hold the candle securely. Starting at one side or end, draw the embossing tool over the surface of the candle with a firm, even pressure. Do not remove the tool from the surface of the candle until or unless you are changing directions.
3. Warm the tool as needed and continue until the pattern has been formed in the wax.

DISTRESSED SURFACE

This method of melting the wax just on the surface of the candle leaves a distressed pattern behind. This can sometimes be useful if you are unable to remove a seam line on a candle—perhaps left from molding a candle in an orange juice can—and would like to disguise the seam. Using a hair dryer on a high setting, blow on the surface of the candle until the wax "weeps." Turn the candle as you work until the entire surface has been distressed in this way.

CARVING

Carving is a technique that works best on overdipped candles because it allows the colors underneath to be revealed. Contrasting colors work best if you are going to be carving the candle.

materials

Overdipped paraffin or beeswax candle

equipment

Linoleum- or wood-carving tool with changeable blades

instructions

1. Depending on the tool you are using, you can achieve a variety of designs by carving. One

Two's Company, Mount Vernon, New York

of the easiest things to do is to "stripe" a candle from top to bottom, exposing the color underneath. Choose a blade that digs into the surface and creates a design you like.

2. Hold the candle firmly braced against your body. Using the cutting tool, take firm, even strokes with the tool, cutting away from your body and always to the same depth (photo 7).

3. Turn the candle as you cut until the desired design is completed.

FREE-HAND CARVING

Free-hand carving can be fun. It is not difficult if you stay with simple, familiar patterns like stars, commas, or crescent moons. Try a few practice cuts in the bottom of the candle before you start.

WAX APPLIQUÉ

There are many molds available that can be used for appliqué. The requirements for these molds are simply that they be shallow and not too large for the candle surface. In addition to appliqué molds, you can make rolled appliqués to slice and "glue" on candles. Whipped wax is another method of appliqué.

MOLDED APPLIQUÉ

Choose appliqué molds that are visually appealing to you. Improvised molds should be able to be poured to a shallow depth and still show the design. Many candy molds are perfect for appliqué molds. Appliqués can also be painted after they are applied to the candle for an added effect.

materials

Appliqué mold
Paraffin wax, 140° F (60° C) melting point
Sculpture wax or tacky micro wax

equipment

Wax melter
Spoon or ladle
Disposable pie plate
Ice cream stick or old paintbrush
Small can

instructions

1. Choose a mold. Heat the wax to the correct temperature for the mold (see page 54).
2. Pour or ladle the wax into the appliqué mold. Allow the wax to cool.
3. Choose one of the three methods below to affix the appliqué.

    Method #1: Allow the wax to cool completely in the mold. Remove the appliqué from the mold. Place a disposable pie plate on a warm burner. Place the appliqué on its back just long enough to melt a thin layer of wax on the back of the mold. Quickly affix it to the candle, holding it in place until the wax has hardened.

Method #2: Allow the wax to cool completely in the mold. Remove the appliqué from the mold. Melt some sculpture wax or tacky microcrystalline wax in a small can. With an ice cream stick or an old paintbrush, paint some of the melted wax on the back of the appliqué mold. Affix the appliqué to the candle quickly and hold firmly in place until the wax has cooled.

Method #3: Melt some sculpture wax or tacky microcrystalline wax in a small can. Allow the wax to cool in the mold until it can be removed but is still warm and somewhat flexible. Remove the appliqué from the mold. Using an ice cream stick or old paintbrush, paint the back with some of the melted wax. Affix the appliqué to the candle and hold firmly in place until the wax has cooled. This is the best method if you are putting a large flat appliqué on a round candle.

WHIPPED WAX

Create old-fashioned snowball candles or dress up homemade or store-bought candles with this simple technique, which is enjoyable for adults and children alike.

An example of a whipped wax candle; Two's Company, Mount Vernon, New York

materials

Paraffin wax, 140° F (60° C) melting point

Candle

Candle dye

equipment

Wax melter

Small dish

Fork

Blunt knife

instructions

1. Melt a small amount of wax and pour it into a dish. If you wish, add candle dye to color the wax. Using a fork, whip the wax until it becomes thick and foamy (photos 8 through 10). This may take five minutes or more.

2. The whipped wax must be applied while it is warm. You have a limited amount of time to work with it, but do not panic. If the wax cools too much, you can simply melt it down and begin again.

3. Use the end of a knife and dip it into the whipped wax. Apply the wax generously to the surface of the candle as you would apply icing to a cake (photo 11). Start in one area on the candle's surface, cover it completely, then move on. To create snow, the whipped wax must be applied heavily.

ROLLED APPLIQUÉ

Rolled appliqués are not rolled at all—they just look like it. They are formed in the same way as tapers and making them can be addictive! These appliqués are most effective when done in vibrant colors and are a great way to use up colored wax.

materials

Paraffin candle

Colored wax in several colors

Flat-braided wick

equipment

Double boiler (several small cans placed in a wide, shallow pan)

Sharp knife

Small pot

Stone Candles, Berkeley, California

instructions

1. Fill the double boiler with water. Place a different colored wax in each can. Choose one or two light colors and as many other colors as you have room for in your double boiler. Remember that vibrant colors will work best for this technique, so add a little extra dye if necessary.

2. Heat the water until all the colored wax is melted (photo 12). Cut short lengths (about 6 inches or 15 cm) of flat-braided wick or reuse an old wick.

3. Dip the wick into a color repeatedly until a layer of wax builds up (photo 13, page 113). Go to another color and repeat, varying the number of dips so that each layer is a different width. Continue dipping, alternating light and dark colors, until you have a built-up wax about the width of a taper or a little larger.

4. Pull the wick from one end of the wax; do not pull it all the way out, but about halfway (photo 14). The wick should pull out and offer no resistance.

5. Boil water in the small pot. Warm the knife in the water. Starting on the end of the wax without wick in it, slice off a thin layer of wax and immediately place it on the surface of the candle (photo 15). Continue working in this way, placing the wax slices on the candle (photo 16).

6. Should the wax begin to get too hard to work with, suspend it for about 15 seconds in heated wax of the last color it was dipped in. This should soften the wax sufficiently. (This is why you always leave a little wick intact until you get to the very end of the wax.)

7. Pull the wick out as needed and continue slicing and placing the wax until the surface of the candle is covered. For a really interesting effect, use several different wax sticks for each candle.

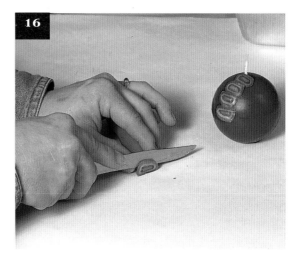

oriental facts

In the Orient, wax for candlemaking was obtained from the candleberry and the tallow tree.

MISCELLANEOUS SURFACE TECHNIQUES

APPLYING PRESSED FLOWERS AND LEAVES

Pressed botanical materials give any candle a softer look. Pressing flowers and leaves is a good summertime activity and the pressed materials can be stored away until you are ready to use them.

I like to have on hand a good sampling of sizes, shapes, and colors so that I can usually find what I need when the opportunity arises.

Pressing botanical materials need not be complicated or time consuming. Small commercially made presses are available and will suit most people's needs. If you cannot find a press, you can improvise one easily. Buy thick, absorbent paper and layer it between thin sheets of plywood. Using

Avid Press, New Paltz, New Jersey

Nature's Creations, Creedmoor, North Carolina

a cement block or other heavy object for weight accomplishes the same objective as a press.

Many types of leaves can be pressed between the pages of a telephone book, but because of their nectar, flowers need more absorbent paper than the newsprint found in phone books. Many flowers press well—all you have to do is lay them out flat on the paper. Still others will need to be pulled apart; the components are pressed separately and reassembled on the candle. Under normal conditions, most flowers need not stay in the press longer than two weeks.

materials

Paraffin or beeswax candle

Pressed flowers and/or leaves

Toothpick

Piece of white paper

Pencil

Craft glue

Spray sealer or liquid matte finish*

*optional

instructions

1. Assemble your flowers or leaves on a work surface. On a scrap of paper, sketch an outline the size and shape of the candle surface to be covered. Arrange the botanicals on the paper until you come up with an arrangement that is pleasing to the eye.

2. To transfer the pressed materials to the candle, turn over the pieces one at a time in the order in which they will be affixed. With a toothpick, place a small dot of glue along the outside edges and several dots in the center of the pressed materials. It is not necessary to smear the entire botanical with glue, but use enough to keep it in place.

3. Position each botanical on the candle and apply firm, even pressure with your fingers until all the glue has been smoothed out underneath. Continue applying the materials in this fashion until you have created your arrangement. Allow the glue to dry several hours. If you wish, you may spray the surface with a sealing agent similar to that used for dried floral arrangements or cover it with a liquid matte finish.

CANDLES ROLLED IN HERBS OR FLOWERS

Plain or undecorated candles can be given an wonderfully natural look by covering the surface with ground or pulverized herbs and spices or flow-ers. Cinnamon, cloves, sage, lavender flowers, tumeric, or paprika can be used, to name only a few. The candle pictured here was rolled in dried laven-der flowers.

materials

candle

white craft glue

ground or pulverized herbs, spices, or flowers

small dish with flat bottom

equipment

paintbrush

instructions

1. Cover half the candle's surface (one side of the candle) with white craft glue.

2. Sprinkle the herbs or flowers in the dish. Roll the candle back and forth across the dish until the glued surface is covered. Repeat this procedure with the other side of the candle.

seven angels

In the Jewish mystical tradition, the Menorah, a candelabrum used in worship, is symbolic of the seven celestial bodies and seven archangels: Cassiel or Saturn, the keeper of secrets; Gabriel or the Moon, the spirit of strength; Haniel or Venus, the spirit of splendor; Madimial or Mars, the spirit of those who make red; Michael or the Sun, who is unto God; Raphael or Mercury, the spirit of healing; and Zadkiel or Jupiter, the spirit of justice.

3. Finish by filling in the stubborn bare spots. Apply glue to the bare areas with a paintbrush and press the flowers, herb, or spice on the candle by hand. This works best if done after the first applications have dried.

WAX METALLIC FINISH

Wax metallic finish is used on candles that have raised surfaces or scenes on their surfaces. The coat of color brings attention to the candle's contours by making them more visible and attractive. Apply the finish to the raised surface with your fingers, paintbrush, or cloth, and allow to dry. When it dries, buff it with a soft cloth to develop the sheen. Candles decorated in this way can be burned as usual.

SPRAY-PAINT FINISHES

Spray-paint finishes are often sold as candle-making accessories. The two most commonly offered are metallic paints and pearl luster paint. These spray paints are high quality and are used to completely cover the candle surface with color. Metallic sprays leave a glossy, hard-looking surface on the candle. Pearl luster sprays leave a soft, fuzzy overall texture with sparkling highlights.

METALLIC TAPE

Metallic tapes are available for trimming the edges of candles. When buying metallic tapes, be sure that they are self adhesive and are formulated to adhere to a wax surface. Metallic tapes give a formal, finished look to any candle to which they are applied.

*trouble*shooting

Potpourri-infused molded candles and container candles by Illuminée du Monde, Bristol, Vermont

Bright Lights, Lower Lake, California

When learning a new craft, we all make mistakes, and candlemaking is no exception. It requires considerable practice and patience to successfully make some of the candles in this book. Over time you will develop a "touch" when working with the wax that will enable you to be a good candlemaker and a good troubleshooter.

However, standard types of candles develop more predictable problems and most of these are easily overcome after experiencing them one or two times. This section is designed to help the beginner sort out the problem when something does go wrong.

Problem #1:

The candle will not release from the mold.

Causes:

- Wax built up on the insides of the mold above the height of the poured candle.
- The mold type does not permit easy release.
- The well was overfilled when the candle was topped off.
- If the mold is metal, it may be dented.
- Poor-quality wax was used or the wax was too soft.
- The candle cooled too slowly.

Solutions:

- Use only beeswax in pop-out molds or in combination with paraffin wax for molded candles.
- Do not fill melted wax beyond the hardened wax in your molds.

- Store molds in original pack-aging; purchase a new mold.
- Buy quality waxes from a rep-utable source; beware of extremely inexpensive wax and additives.
- Use a cool-water bath for most molded candles (see individual instructions).

Problem #2:

There are cracks or fractures inside the candle.

Causes:
- The candle cooled too quickly after pouring
- The well in the candle was topped off after the wax in the mold hardened.

Solutions:
- Do not use a cool-water bath for beeswax candles; cool the candle in a covered con-tainer.
- Watch for a well to develop as the candle cools, and fill it immediately.

Problem #3:

There is mottling on the outside of the candle.

Causes:
- Old wax that had been reheated too many times was used.
- There is high oil content in the wax.
- Candle allowed to cool too slowly.

Stone Candles, Berkeley, California

Solutions:
- Use fresh wax; buy high-quality ingredients and waxes.
- Use a cool-water bath to cool candles more quickly.

Problem #4:

There are air bubbles on the surface of the candle.

Causes:
- The mold was not tapped to rid it of air pockets.
- There was dust in the mold.
- The candle was poured too quickly.
- There was water in the mold.

Let There Be Light, Asheville, North Carolina

Solutions:

- Tap the mold with a wooden spoon to rid it of air pockets before placing it in a cool-water bath.

- Keep molds stored in the original packaging when not in use.

- Pour the candle slowly and evenly.

- Make sure that the inside of the mold is dry before pouring the candle.

Problem #5:

There are frost marks on the candle.

Causes:

- The mold was too cold when the candle was poured.

- The wax was not hot enough when the candle was poured.

- The candle was removed from the mold too early.

Solutions:

- Warm the outside of the mold with hot tap water before pouring the candle.

- Measure the temperature of the wax with a reliable thermometer; bring the wax to the proper pouring temperature.

- Be certain that the candle is completely cooled before trying to remove it from the mold.

Problem #6:

The candle caved in on the side.

Causes:

- The surface tension around the wick was not released by piercing (until the wax hardened too much).

Solutions:

- Pierce the wax on the well as it forms, before it hardens completely; make sure that you pierce the wax all along the length of the wick.

Problem #7:

There are bubbled lines around the circumference of the candle.

Causes:

- The water level in the cool-water bath was not at the level of the wax in the mold.

Solutions:

- Make sure that the water bath can accommodate the entire length of the candle.

D. L. Hill, Salt Lake City, Utah

Problem #8:

The flame burns a hole down through the candle, leaving a rim of unmelted wax around the outside.

Causes:

- The wick is too small for the diameter of the candle.
- Wax additives are slowing the burning of the candle so much that the wick selected is too small for the wax formulation.
- Too much stearin or additive to slow the burning was used.

Solutions:

- Do not overuse additives that lengthen the burning time of the candle.
- Use the proper wick for the diameter candle you are making.

Problem #9:

There is excessive smoking.

Causes:

- The wick is too large for the candle.
- There is a draft in the room.
- Trim the wick to a maximum of 1 inch (2.5 cm).

Solutions:

- Use the proper size wick for the candle's diameter.
- Do not burn candles in a strong draft.

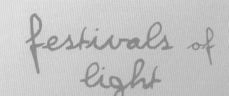

Let There Be Light, Asheville, North Carolina.

- The Indian festival "Diwali" is dedicated to the goddess of wealth, Lakshmi. Participants burn a candle or lamp to invite good fortune.
- "Walpurgis Night" in Germany, associated with witchcraft, is a relic of pagan May Day celebrations when torches were lit.
- When Halloween was first celebrated, it was associated with witchcraft, and participants carried candles or torches.
- Birthday candles are a beloved part of birthdays, which are, in fact, celebrations of the passing of another year.

Candles courtesy of Earth Guild, Asheville, North Carolina

Problem #10:

The wick snuffs itself out in the melted wax.

Causes:

- The wick is too small to take up the molten wax.
- The wrong wick type was used.

Solutions:

- Use the proper size wick for the diameter candle you are making.
- Use the proper wick for the type of candle you are making.

Problem #11:

The candle drips excessively.

Causes:

- The wick is not properly centered in the candle.
- The wax is too soft.
- There is a draft in the room.
- The wick is too small for the diameter of the candle.
- The wick is too small for the wax formulation of the candle.

Solutions:

- Use wick-centering spiders or be sure to center the wick properly.
- Buy high-quality waxes.
- Do not burn candles in drafty rooms.
- Use the proper size wick for the candle diameter you are making.

Problem #12:

The candle sputters.

Causes:

- There are impurities on the wick.
- There is water on the wick.
- There is water in the wax around the wick (common in ice candles).

Solutions:

- Do not use crayons to color candles; use clean wax free of debris.
- Prime all wicks before making the candle; keep wicks sealed in plastic to keep out moisture when not in use.
- Allow water candles to dry thoroughly before burning them.

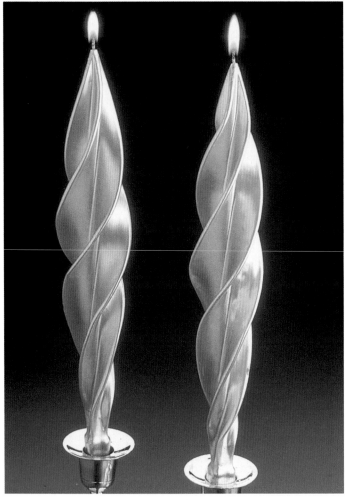

Two's Company, Mount Vernon, New York

Problem #13:

The wick lights poorly.

Causes:

- The wick is wet (common in water and ice candles).
- There is mold sealer on the wick.
- The wick was not primed.

Solutions:

- Use clean, dry wick; prime all wicks.
- Clean all mold sealer off the wick before lighting the candle.

Problem #14:

Container candles smoke excessively.

Causes:

- The wick is too large for the candle diameter.

Solutions:

- Use proper size wick for the diameter of the container used.

Problem #15:

There is wax left on the sides of the container.

Causes:

- The candle burned for short periods of time.
- The melting point of the wax was not low enough.

Solutions:

- Burn container candles for several hours at a time.
- Use the correct wax formulation for all container candles as indicated on page 47.

Crafted by Kaeran Dykes and staff, Dollywood, Pigeon Forge, Tennessee

acknowledgements

We would like to thank Pourette Manufacturing Company (Seattle, Washington), and the Candlewick Company (New Britain, Pennsylvania) for generously donating materials for the book. Also, special thanks to Jane and Scott Taylor, and Marianne Ralbovsky.

For donating candles, we would like to extend our gratitude to Let There Be Light, Sue Techow, Illuminée du Monde, Patti Hill, Angel Lady Designs, Dollywood, Stone Candles, Two's Company, Nature's Creations, Susan Schadt Designs, Bright Lights, Avid Press, Keepsake Candles, Pei-Ling Becker, and Hill Enterprises West.

For assistance with photography props, thanks to Natural Home, The Loft, and TS Morrison Company, all in Asheville, North Carolina. And finally, thanks to Miegan Gordon and Dana Irwin for lending us their candlesticks.

index